Japanese Monograph No. 134

BURMA OPERATIONS RECORD
15TH ARMY OPERATIONS IN IMPHAL AREA
AND WITHDRAWAL TO NORTHERN BURMA

(Revised Edition)

PREPARED BY
HEADQUARTERS
UNITED STATES ARMY, JAPAN

DISTRIBUTED BY
OFFICE OF THE CHIEF OF MILITARY HISTORY
DEPARTMENT OF THE ARMY

Published by Books Express Publishing
Copyright © Books Express, 2011
ISBN 978-1-78039-086-4

Books Express publications are available from all good retail and online booksellers. For publishing proposals and direct ordering please contact us at: info@books-express.com

Foreword

This record was compiled by Mr. Jiso Yamaguchi, a member of the Report and Statistical Section of the Demobilization Bureau and former major of the Southern Army Staff Section. The material is based mainly on the recollections of the following persons: Ex-Maj. Gen. Renya Mutaguchi, former commander of the 15th Army; ex-Lt. Cols. Bun Hirai, Iwaichi Fujiwara, Seizaburo Usui, and Iwao Takahashi, former staff officers of the 15th Army; ex-Lt. Col. Takeshi Kuwabara, former staff officer of the 15th Division; ex-Maj. Gen. Tsuchitaro Kawada, former commander of the 31st Division; ex-Maj. Yuzo Miura, former staff officer of the 33d Division; ex-Col. Kuniji Kato, former chief of staff of the 31st Division; and ex-Maj. Tsutomu Sakamoto, former staff officer of the 53d Division.

10 October 1952

Revised Edition

Many former officers, having knowledge of the Imphal Operation, have assisted the Foreign Histories Division to fill in the numerous gaps and to correct the errors in the original study. We acknowledge our indebtedness and express our thanks to the following former officers of the Imperial Japanese Army:

    General Kawabe, CG, Burma Area Army
    Lt. Gen. Sato, CG, 31st Division
    Maj. Gen. Hayashi, 24th Mixed Brigade
    Maj. Gen. Katakura, C/S, 33d Army
    Maj. Gen. Okada, C/S, 15th Division
    Maj. Gen. Yamamoto, CG, 33d Infantry Group
    Col. Fuwa, Staff, Burma Area Army
    Col. Hashimoto, Staff, 15th Army
    Col. Kushida, Staff, Southern Army
    Col. Matsumura, CO, 60th Infantry Regiment
    Col. Nukui, CO, 213th Infantry Regiment
    Col. Omoto, CO, 51st Infantry Regiment
    Col. Sakuma, CO, 214th Infantry Regiment
    Col. Torikai, CO, 138th Infantry Regiment
    Lt. Col. Horiba, Staff, 33d Division
    Lt. Col. Kikkawa, Staff, Southern Army
    Maj. Ito, CO, 3d Battalion, 213th Infantry
    Maj. Masuda, CO, 2d Battalion, 124th Infantry
    Maj. Miura, Staff, 33d Division

Maj. Morimoto, CO, 1st Battalion, 58th Infantry
Maj. Ogata, Staff, 5th Air Division
Maj. Shoji, Staff, 53d Division

We are also indebted to General Kawabe, Commanding General of the Burma Area Army and Major General Miyazaki, Commanding General of the 31st Infantry Group for the use of their diaries. Operations records of the 15th and 31st Divisions, compiled by Colonel Matsumura and Lt. Col. Yamaki, respectively, were also of great value in supplying dates and other material not included in the original version of the Monograph. Essential data were also obtained from the record of the Imphal Operation, recently compiled by the Staff College, Japanese Self Defense Force, and casualty lists were furnished by the First Demobilization Bureau of the Japanese Government.

10 October 1957

Preface

Through Instructions No. 126 to the Japanese Government, 12 October 1945, subject: Institution for War Records Investigation, steps were initiated to exploit military historical records and official reports of the Japanese War Ministry and Japanese General Staff. Upon dissolution of the War Ministry and the Japanese General Staff, and the transfer of their former functions to the Demobilization Bureau, research and compilation continued and developed into a series of historical monographs.

The paucity of original orders, plans and unit journals, which are normally essential in the preparations of this type of record, most of which were lost or destroyed during field operations or bombing raids rendered the task of compilation most difficult; particularly distressing has been the complete lack of official strength reports, normal in AG or G3 records. However, while many of the important orders, plans and estimates have been reconstructed from memory and therefore are not textually identical with the originals, they are believed to be generally accurate and reliable.

Under the supervision of the Demobilization Bureau, the basic material contained in this monograph was compiled and written in Japanese by former officers, on duty in command and staff units within major units during the period of operations. Translation was effected through the facilities of Allied Translators and Interpreters Service, G2, General Headquarters, Far East Command.

This Japanese Operational Monograph was rewritten in English by the Japanese Research Division, Military History Section, Headquarters, Far East Command and is based on the translation of the Japanese original. Editorial corrections were limited to those necessary for coherence and accuracy.

Revised Edition

Originally rewritten and edited in October 1952, this monograph was completely revised in 1957. During the intervening five year period, a tremendous amount of additional information had been developed through research. Provided with the new material, it has been possible to correct many inaccuracies and fill in a number of gaps. Map coverage in the revised edition has also been expanded and improved.

This revision was accomplished by the Foreign Histories Division, Office of the Military History Officer, Headquarters, United States Army Japan, the successor to the original editing agency. Reorganization of the text and editorial corrections were accomplished in an effort to improve the historical value of the manuscript while still retaining the Japanese viewpoint.

10 October 1957

TABLE OF CONTENTS

Chapter		Page
1.	15th ARMY ORGANIZATION AND OPERATIONS AFTER THE SUBJUGATION OF BURMA.	1
	Enemy Situation in Burma Area.	3
	Air Situation in Burma	5
	Counterattack on Akyab by British-Indian Forces.	6
	Invasion of Northern Burma by the Wingate Brigade.	7
	Dispersal of the Wingate Brigade.	8
	Objectives of the Wingate Invasion.	9
	Results of the Wingate Invasion	9
	Intelligence Information on Enemy Operations	10
	Plans for Operation No. 21	13
	Reorganization of Northern Burma Defense	14
	Operations and Reconnaissance West of the Chindwin River	18
	Planning for Operation "Bu".	21
	Redisposition of 33d Division.	22
	Organization of the 31st Division.	24
2.	PLANS AND PREPARATIONS FOR THE INVASION OF EASTERN INDIA	27
	Preliminary Planning for Operations in India	27
	Map Maneuver at Rangoon	29
	Development of Imphal Operation Plans	32

Chapter		Page
2.	Preliminary Planning for Operations in India (contd.)	
	Policy of Imperial General Headquarters Toward India.	35
	Enemy Situation in September 1943	36
	Final Imphal Operation Planning.	37
	Southern Army Order for Preparations.	37
	Burma Area Army Strategic Plan.	38
	15th Army Tactical Plan.	39
	Acceleration of Logistic Preparations	42
	Relations with the Indian National Army	47
	Intelligence Collecting Plan	50
	Operations in the Salween River Area	51
	15th Army Operational Plan.	51
	Blockade of Salween River Crossings	53
	Chin Hills Operations of the 33d Division.	55
	33d Division Operational Plan	56
	Advancing of Forward Positions.	57
	Hukawng Operations of the 18th Division.	59
	Concentration of Forces.	60
	Suspension of the Offensive	61
	Establishment of the Taihpa Ga Defense.	64
	Withdrawal to the Maingkwan Area.	64
	Retreat to the Jambu Hkintang Mountains	65

Chapter		Page
2.	Hukawng Operations of the 18th Division (contd.)	
	Defense in the Shaduzup Area.	67
	Conclusion of the Hukawng Operation	69
	Preparations for the Imphal Operation.	69
	15th Division.	69
	31st Division	71
	33d Division.	73
	Enemy Situation in Early 1944.	74
	Estimate of Situation	76
	Final Plans for the Imphal Operations.	76
	Approval by Imperial General Headquarters.	77
	15th Army Attack Orders.	79
	Tactical Considerations	84
	Concealment of Intentions	85
	Operations Plan of the 15th Division	86
	Task Force Organization	86
	Attack Order.	87
	Operations Plan of the 31st Division	88
	Task Force Organization	89
	Attack Order.	90
	Operations Plan of the 33d Division.	90
	Task Force Organization..	90
	Attack Order.	92

Chapter	Page
3. THE IMPHAL OPERATION.	94
The Wingate Airborne Invasion.	94
Start of the Imphal Offensive.	97
The 33d Division - March and April	97
Operations in the Tonzang Area.	99
Encirclement of the Enemy	101
Suggested Suspension of Offensive	103
Drive Toward Tengnoupal	104
Operations Toward Bishenpur	108
The 15th Division - March and April.	112
Cutting the Northern Approaches to Imphal . .	112
Attacks on Sengmai.	115
Redeployment East of the Iril River	116
Enemy Counterattacks on the Division Rear . .	117
The 31st Division - March and April.	118
Attack on Sangshak.	119
Occupation of Kohima.	119
Attempts to Cut the Kohima-Dimapur Road . . .	122
Units Ordered to Imphal	123
Assumption of the Defensive	125
The 33d Division - May and June.	125
Operations Against Bishenpur.	125
The Torbung Roadblock	127

Chapter		Page
3.	The 33d Division – May and June (contd.)	
	Division Commander Relieved.	128
	Attack on Bishenpur Renewed.	129
	Enemy Withdrawal from Torbung.	131
	Change in Balance of Power	131
	Suspension of the Offensive.	132
	The 15th Division – May and June.	133
	Enemy Infiltration Tactics	135
	Attempts to Consolidate Positions.	136
	Retreat of the 31st Division	136
	Withdrawal to the Sangshak Area.	137
	Offensive Abandoned.	139
	The 31st Division – May and June.	139
	General Offensive by the Enemy	141
	Decision to Withdraw.	142
	Operations Against the Wingate Airborne Force . . .	144
	Activation of the 33d Army	146
	Employment of the 53d Division	147
	Results of the Wingate Invasion.	149
	Withdrawal from Imphal.	150
	Redisposition of the 15th Army	150
	The Palel Offensive.	151

Chapter	Page
4. WITHDRAWAL FROM EASTERN INDIA.	155
Suspension of the Imphal Operation.	155
Withdrawal to the Chindwin River.	157
Withdrawal to the Zibyu Range	160
Line of Communications.	163
Operations in Northern Burma.	166
Command Changes and Plans for the "Ban" Operation.	167
Final Plans for the Irrawaddy Battle.	173
15th Army Situation Prior to the Irrawaddy River Withdrawal.	178
Withdrawal to the Irrawaddy Defense Line.	181
Logistics in the 15th Army Withdrawal	185
Construction of Irrawaddy Defense Positions	186

MAPS AND CHARTS

MAPS

No.	Title	Page
1.	Disposition of 15th Army 1 December 1942	2
2.	Plan for Operation No. 21 1942	12
3.	General Plan of Supply System for Imphal Operation	34
4.	Proposed Road Construction for Imphal Operation	43
5.	Salween Operation Fall 1943	52
6.	Operation of 33d Division in the Chin Hills Area	54
7.	Concentration of 18th Division - Hukawng Valley	58
8a.	Hukawng Operation - 18th Division	62
8b.	Hukawng Operation - 18th Division	63
9.	Progress of Deployment - 31st & 15th Divisions	68
10.	Imphal Operation Plan - 15th and 31st Divisions	81
11.	Imphal Operation Plan - 33d Division	83
12.	Operations of 33d Division - Tonzang Area	98
13.	Operational Progress of Yamamoto Detachment	106
14.	Operations, 33d Division - Moirang to Bishenpur	109
15.	Operational Progress - 15th Division March - April 1944	113
16.	Operational Progress - 31st Division	120
17.	Operations of 33d Division - Bishenpur Area	126
18.	Operational Progress - 15th Division May - July 1944	134

MAPS (contd.)

No.	Title	Page
19.	Operations of 31st Division - Kohima	140
20.	Operations Against Enemy Airborne Force	145
21.	Logistical Disposition - 15th Army	184

General Reference

I.	Progress of Withdrawal from Imphal	189
II.	Withdrawal Operation to Irrawaddy River - 15 Army	191

CHARTS

No.	Title	Page
1.	Logistic Units to Support the Imphal Operation	46
2.	Accumulation of Munitions Prior to Imphal Operation	48
3.	Personnel Losses of 15th Army in the Imphal Operation	164

CHAPTER 1

15TH ARMY ORGANIZATION AND OPERATIONS AFTER THE
SUBJUGATION OF BURMA

After the completion of the Burma subjugation operations in the summer of 1942, the 15th Army, in compliance with a request of the Southern Army, conducted a study regarding the possibility of offensive operations in the direction of eastern India. At this time, however, the primary mission of the 15th Army was the securing of Burma and the eastern India offensive never went beyond the planning stage.

The security line assigned to the 15th Army extended from Pingka through Lameng, Tengchung and Myitkyina to Kamaing in the east, and from Kalewa to Akyab in the west. The Southern Army commander ordered that any invasion operations to be launched eastward across the Salween River or across the India-Burma border would first be approved by him.

In the summer of 1942 the 15th Army was composed of the 18th, 33d, 55th and 56th Divisions. Following the operational period, each division made basic changes in disposition with a view to establishing a permanent defensive setup in accordance with the Army's primary mission. (Map No.1). The new dispositions were calculated to define the defense responsibilities of each division and allow for the readjustment, training, and recovery of the Army units after completion

MAP NO. 1

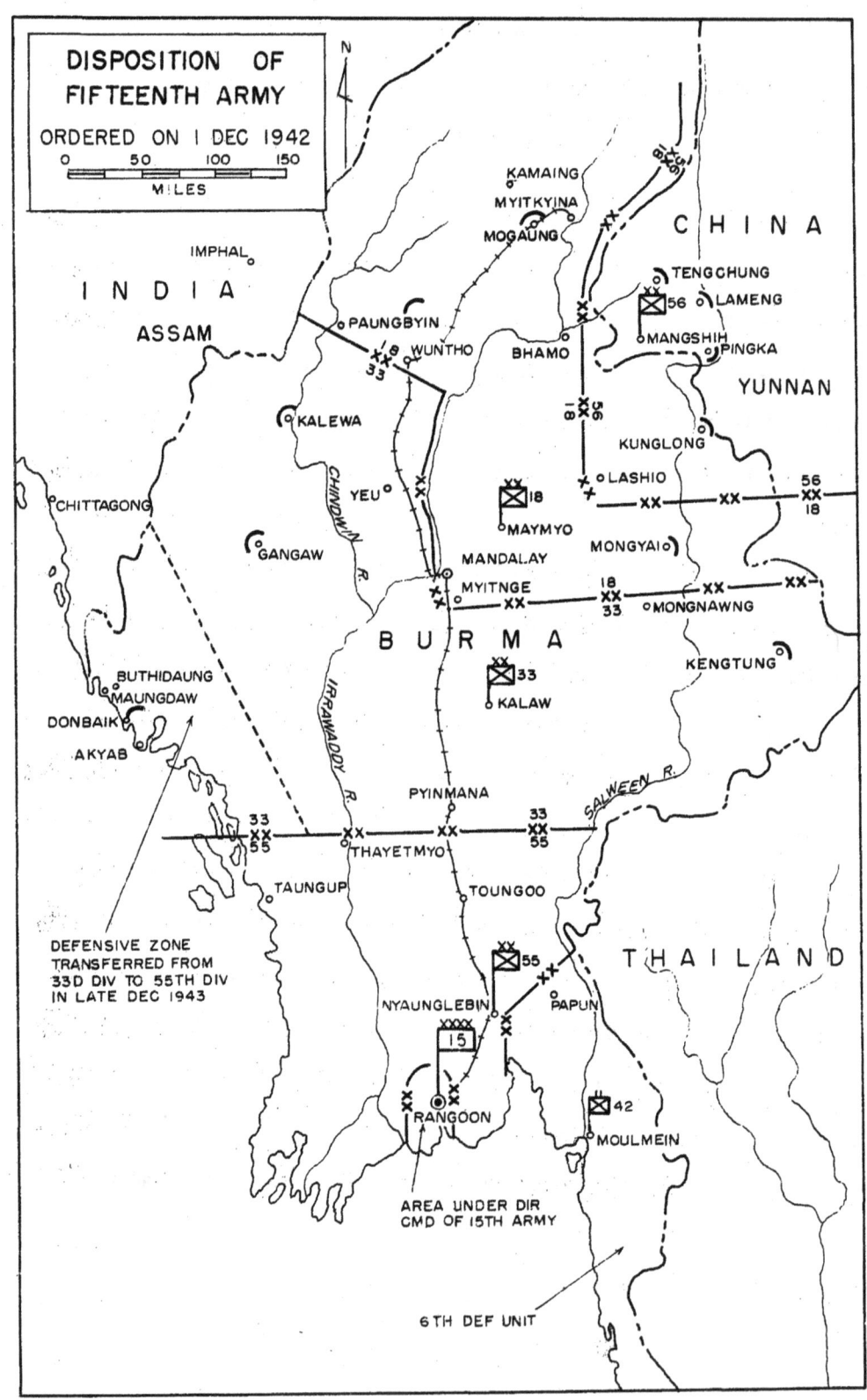

of the subjugation operations. It was generally concluded that for both sides large scale movements, particularly the operation of large mechanized, United States and British forces, would be difficult in northern Burma and especially in the area north and west of the line linking Myitkyina, Mogaung, Zibyu Mountain Range, Kalewa and the India-Burma border.

Enemy Situation in Burma Area

The enemy was put to rout by the 15th Army as far as India and the sector east of the Salween River in the Yunnan province of China. The British-Indian forces in the area of the Mayu Peninsula northwest of Akyab fled to Chittagong by land and sea without offering any resistance, while the British-Indian forces in the Manipur area abandoned heavy equipment, intermingled with the refugees, and fled to eastern Assam. Meanwhile, the 38th, 96th and 200th Divisions of the Chungking Army, with the retreat route to the Yunnan Province blocked at Lashio and Myitkyina, had fled through the Hukawng Valley to Ledo in Assam. The main force of the Chinese Yunnan Expeditionary Army had abandoned its equipment in the sector west of the Salween River to flee to the Paoshan area. Enemy defense measures in Manipur, Assam and Yunnan were practically non-existent and it was believed that it would be almost impossible for the enemy to reorganize.

The Indian government was concerned over the delicate anti-British political situation within the country. The widespread oppression of leaders of the National Congress faction conducted in Bombay in August 1942, the recognition of a crisis by the leaders of the British Empire, and bitter disputes over the problem of dealing with the refugees and remnants of the vanquished troops were indicative of the uneasy political situation.

It was estimated that large scale counterattacks by the enemy would be restricted to the following established routes of operation: in the coastal area, the Cox's Bazar-Donbaik-Akyab Road; in the mountain area, the Aijal-Haka-Gangaw Road, the Silchar-Bishenpur Road, and the Dimapur-Kohima-Imphal-Kalewa Road. Except for the coastal road and Dimapur-Imphal Road, these routes were usable only during the dry season and the enemy would have to improve the routes of operation before conducting a counterattack in the west.

The heights of the Arakan Range offered a barrier to a counterattack in the western sector of Burma and the Chindwin River and Zibyu Mountain Range were further obstacles to the enemy operations. It was quite probable that the enemy would try to invade northern Burma from the Ledo area to reopen the India-China overland route, but it was considered almost impossible to construct a road that would be usable by motor vehicles, in both dry and rainy seasons, in the Tanai River bed which was the operational route from Ledo. The speed with which the Chinese New 1st Army was being organized near Tinsukia and its strength were considered to be vital factors in estimating the enemy's future plans in the Ledo area.

From Yunnan Province the Chungking Army would be faced with steep mountains and the Salween River, as well as a lack of transportation facilities and the exhaustion of local supply sources. Since the Chungking Army, alone, lacked the combat strength to conduct an effective counterattack, there was little fear of invasion from the east for the time being.

On the basis of the above estimate it was believed that during the remainder of 1942 the enemy would concentrate on establishing defensive measures in preparation for a Japanese attack upon India or China.

Air Situation in Burma

In the fall of 1942 the enemy air force gradually took the offensive in Burma and showed signs of growing rapidly. In contrast, Japanese air power in Burma had dwindled. There had been a considerable force, with the 5th Air Division as the main body. However, with the aggravation of the war situation in the Southeast Pacific area, the 12th Air Brigade (1st and 11th Air Regiments) was transferred to the Southeast Pacific in January 1943 and the 14th Air Regiment was transferred there in February of the same year. This caused a gradual deceleration of air operations against eastern India and Kunming. With enemy air attacks directed mainly on military establishments in Rangoon, Toungoo, Mandalay and Maymyo, the air defense of strategic points in Burma became a matter of grave concern to the Japanese army.

Counterattack on Akyab by British-Indian Forces

At the end of November 1942, the Indian 77th Brigade heading a British-Indian force advanced to the Japanese front line near Maungdaw and Buthidaung. The 15th Army shortened its battle line to extend between Rathedaung and Donbaik and, in the first battle fought since the end of the subjugation campaign, the enemy launched a fierce attack on the Donbaik garrison unit (about one battalion of the 213th Infantry Regiment) in January 1943. The enemy reinforced this front with the British-Indian 7th Division and the attack became more intense. The enemy employment of artillery concentrations and the persistent attacks upon Japanese supply channels by fighter planes was unprecedented.

The 15th Army commander, Lt. Gen. Iida, decided to counterattack by employing the main strength of the 55th Division together with the 213th Infantry Regiment and a part of the mountain artillery of the 33d Division. The Arinobu Detachment (1st Battalion, 213th Regiment, 33d Division) which had marched for about forty days from Pakokku through the steep Arakan Range, advanced to the Kaladan Valley and conducted a surprise attack on the rear of the enemy late in February. The 55th Division commander seized this opportunity to take the offensive and, destroying the enemy main strength in the vicinity of Indin, early in April, recaptured the Maungdaw-Buthidaung area in the beginning of May, driving the enemy back to the India-Burma border.

The intensity of the attack on this front indicated that it was planned as the first movement of the enemy ground counteroffensive against Burma.

Invasion of Northern Burma by the Wingate Brigade

In the middle of February 1943, when the battle in front of Akyab was reaching its climax, 15th Army Headquarters received a report that a British-Indian force of unknown strength had suddenly advanced to the Myitkyina Railway Line between Katha and Shwebo. The force had destroyed the railway at several places and clashed with the Japanese garrison units. The 18th Division and a part of the 33d Division were disposed in the area along the Myitkyina Railway east of the Zibyu Mountain Range. Having placed too much confidence in the barrier formed by that range and the Chindwin River, the Army had omitted reconnaissance of the jungle area in front of the Zibyu Range.

Reports from combat units were conflicting and it was difficult for Army headquarters to grasp the general situation. It gradually became clear that the enemy had crossed the Chindwin River near Paungbyin, and was advancing several columns to the east through the Zibyu Mountain Range. In view of the long overland supply route which would be required, Army headquarters as well as the 18th and 33d Division headquarters originally estimated the enemy force to be a small raiding unit. It developed, however, that the enemy was depending upon air supply, and from the interrogation of prisoners it was determined that the raiding force was the Wingate Brigade which had left Imphal early in January 1943 and advanced east via Palel, Tamu, and Sittaung.

Dispersal of the Wingate Brigade

The 15th Army orders first directed the 18th Division and the 33d Division to contact and destroy the invading enemy. Subsequently information was received that the enemy was crossing the Irrawaddy River and advancing eastward towards Bhamo and Lashio. Elements of the 56th Division were then ordered to participate. By the end of March the enemy was dispersed and turned back toward the Chindwin River. Following the withdrawal, the enemy air supply system failed causing the dispersed groups to invade the native villages to find food and transportation as well as care for the sick and wounded. Many of the enemy were captured or killed by the natives. At the end of May, all of the Wingate force had been driven west of the Chindwin River.

Mopping-up operations in the vast jungle zone were extremely difficult and exhausted the troops and, since such operations had not been anticipated, units lacked the necessary equipment, training and supplies. In addition, units often suffered heavy losses from enemy light automatic weapons in jungle ambuscades. The exhaustion of the men due to inadequate supplies was serious and the Army's plan for restoration of fighting potential and the retraining of troops had to be abandoned.

Objectives of the Wingate Invastion

At first the 15th Army had believed the Wingate Brigade to be a guerrilla unit whose aim was to create confusion and reconnoiter the defense system of the Japanese Army. It was also feared that the group might entirely disrupt the Myitkyina Railway. Later, when elements advanced to the vicinity of Bhamo and Hsipaw, it was thought that the Brigade might be planning to advance to Yunnan to join with the Chungking Army. When the strength of the Brigade became known and it became clear that the main force was not advancing further eastward but was retreating in groups towards the Arakan mountain range, it was clear that the Brigade had other missions. It was later discovered that the Wingate Brigade had been sent to reconnoiter the terrain, to determine the condition of the Japanese Army, to establish an intelligence net, and to study jungle operations in preparation for the next major offensive against northern and central Burma.

Results of the Wingate Invasion

As a result of the Wingate Operations, the 15th Army, which had established comparatively simple defenses, realized that during the dry season the movement of pack horse units in the jungle of northern Burma was unrestricted in many places and that it was easy to cross the Chindwin River by using locally obtainable materials for rafts. The Army had estimated that a counterattack by large enemy groups would be impossible without first repairing the roads and that it would be possible to check small enemy counteroffensives indefinitely if the existing roads and trails leading to India were strongly defended. However, this reasoning was now changed and the change prompted a thorough investigation of the defensive measures employed in central and northern Burma. It was feared that present defenses would collapse if such counterattacks were to be repeated by several echelons of the enemy.[1]

Intelligence Information on Enemy Operations

In April 1943 it was reported that the Allied Forces were transporting Chinese recruits from Kunming to Assam aboard air transports returning from Aid-to-Chiang missions, giving the recruits U.S. equipment and thus reorganizing the Chinese New 1st Army. It was further known that although the strength of the new force was estimated to be

---

1. One vital factor, which did not become known until the Imphal Operations had been launched, was the fact that the United States-Chinese forces and the British-Indian forces in India had made changes in their equipment, training, and combat methods and that they had employed the Wingate Brigade to test the innovations. In addition, the reconnaissance of areas suitable for the construction of airfields, and the establishment of an intelligence net in the jungle zone on the left bank of the Irrawaddy River in central Burma were matters entirely beyond Japanese anticipation. Although it was recognized that such an extensive drive by a tactical brigade into enemy territory, conducting operations unrestrictedly for a long period, was made possible only by air supply, Army and group commanders failed to correct their outdated conceptions of the British-Indian forces and the Chungking Army. Their failure to conceive a counterattack plan based upon the concept of close air-ground cooperation must be considered a great mistake. - <u>Auth</u>.

approximately 10,000, rapid reinforcement was expected. In addition, it was known that they were receiving thorough U.S. style training from U.S. officers at a cadre training center located north of Calcutta, India.

From the Chungking Government sponsored paper, it was learned that the Allied Forces planned to open the Ledo-Mogaung-Myitkyina-Namhkam-Paoshan-Kunming Road (the ancient overland route between India and China). Information was also received that a U.S. force was stationed near Ledo and that the work on the road was already in progress with Ledo as the starting point and Shingbwiyang the terminal.

In the Yunnan area, the Yunnan Expeditionary Army under the command of General Wei Li Huan was being organized, partially equipped and trained by the United States. By April, however, the organization was only about 40 to 50 per cent complete and it was believed that the six or seven divisions were likely to be short of supplies. The Chinese were also planning to transfer certain crack forces as reinforcements to the Yunnan area from other fronts of China.

This intelligence information was interpreted to mean that the expected counteroffensive against Burma would be a large scale three-front drive by British, United States and Chinese forces, with the British-Indian Army advancing from the Arakan front, a U.S. Army unit along the Ledo Road and the Chungking Army from Yunnan Province.

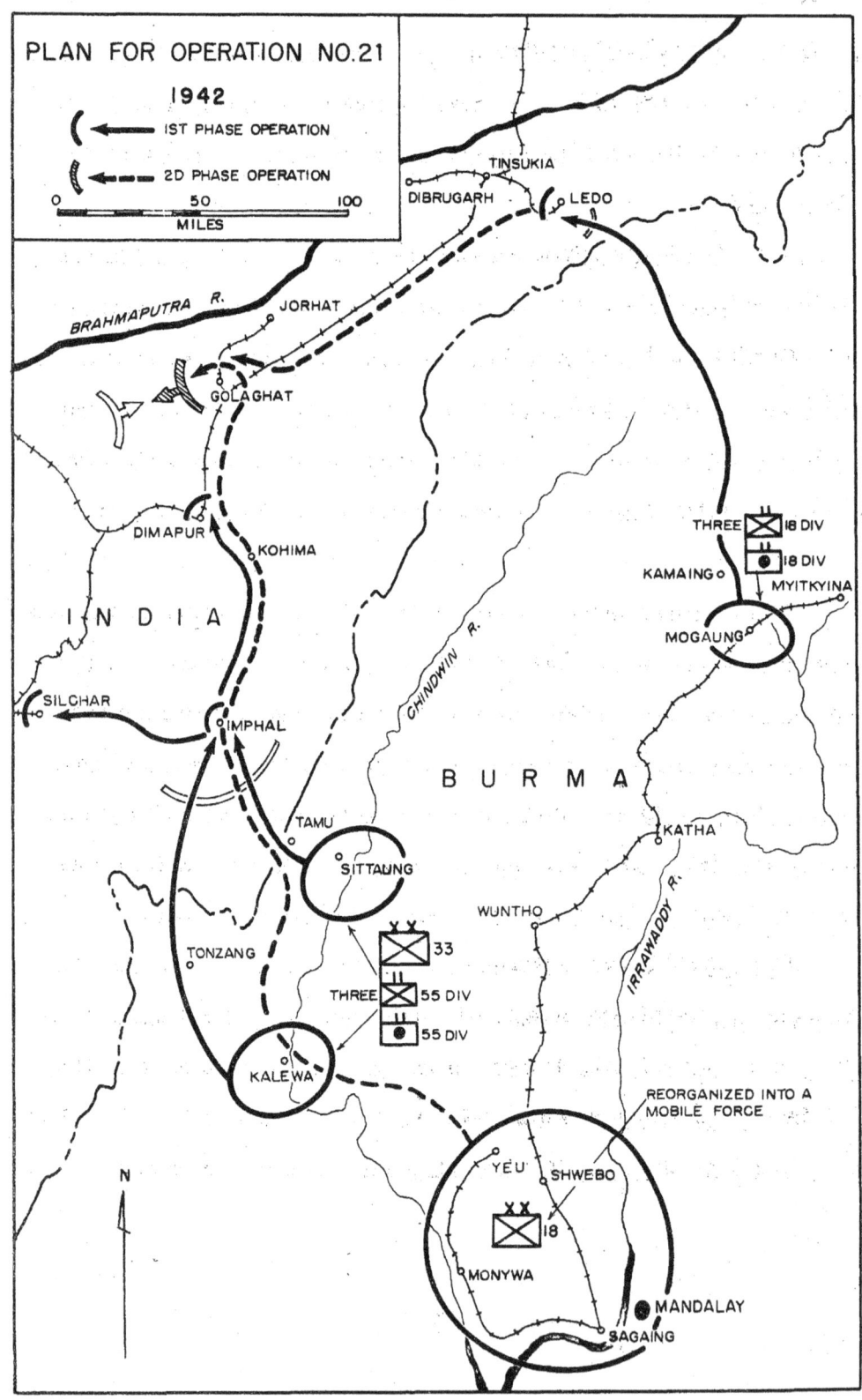

Plans for Operation No. 21

About September 1942, the Southern Army ordered the 15th Army to draft plans for an invasion operation against the Assam area of India. Called Operation No. 21, the objective of the operation was to move into eastern India and take the initiative in implementing a political and strategic India policy following up the success of the Burma subjugation operation.

Briefly, the plan of the operation was as follows: (Map No.2). A leading attack force consisting of the 33d Division reinforced by elements of the 55th Division (then in charge of garrisoning northern Burma) would move along the Kalewa-Imphal-Kohima Dimapur Road, as well as through the mountain area west of the road (including the Chin Hills) and advance to the vicinity of Dimapur and Silchar on the western base of the Arakan Mountain Range. The main force of the 18th Division, reorganized into a mechanized force, would leapfrog the 33d Division and, holding off the anticipated enemy counterattack in the sector west of Dimapur, would advance to the high ground west of Golaghat.

Powerful elements from the 18th Division would be sent to Ledo through the Hukawng area and after destroying the enemy forces there they would advance to and occupy Tinsukia.

The Army would occupy the area around Golaghat, Dimapur and Silchar and, concentrating its main force in the sector west of Golaghat, prepare for the anticipated decisive battle with the enemy forces of the eastern India area.

The 18th Division commander, Lt. Gen. Mutaguchi, at his headquarters in Taunggyi expressed his opinion to the 15th Army commander in early September, stating that the operation would be too difficult in view of the lack of operational preparations in the rear and the lack of time for constructing and repairing the network of roads. Imperial General Headquarters was also doubtful of the results of such an operation and on 23 December 1942 issued a directive suspending the movement of forces of the 15th Army and the accumulation of munitions. The 15th Army was unable to do any large scale work in the rear areas except to conduct the repair of the Shwebo-Kalewa motor vehicle road.

The plan for Operation No. 21 was the first of a series of plans which eventually led to the Imphal Operations.

Reorganization of Northern Burma Defense

In order to coordinate tactical command and political strategy in Burma, an area army headquarters was considered necessary. Accordingly, on 27 March 1943 a directive was issued dictating the new order of battle for the Burma Area Army (commanded by Lt. Gen. Masakazu Kawabe), and revising the order of battle of the 15th Army. The Burma Area Army was to consist of the 15th Army, the 55th Division, and other units to be attached directly to the Area Army. The main force of the 15th Army was to consist of the 18th, 33d, and 56th Divisions as well as the 31st Division (commanded by Lt. Gen. Kotoku Sato) which was to be incorporated upon completion of organization.

The 15th Army Order of Battle was established as follows:

```
CG:     Lt. Gen. Renya Mutaguchi
15th Army HQ
18th Div**
31st Div
33d Div
56th Div**
(15th Div) ..... Assigned October 1943
14th TK Regt
1st AT Arty Bn
6th AT Arty Btry
11th AT Arty Btry
3d Hv Fld Arty Regt (less 2d Bn) ... 150-mm How,
                                     motorized
18th Hv Fld Arty Regt .............. 105-mm Gun,
                                     motorized
21st Hv Fld Arty Bn** .............. 150-mm How,
                                     (horse-drawn)
35th AAA Bn
51st AAA Bn
5th Engr Gp HQ
4th Engr Regt
20th Engr Regt
19th Sig Regt
21st Pon Co
22d Pon Co
26th Pon Co*
10th River-Crossing Material Co*
13th River-Crossing Material Co*
15th River-Crossing Material Co
MP, 15th Army
Logistical units directly under the 15th Army:
    42d Logistical Sector Unit
    5th Fld Trans Gp:
        55th Trk Bn*
        59th Trk Bn
        60th Trk Bn
```

        61st Trk Bn**
        101st Trk Co
        102d Trk Co
        211th Trk Co
        236th Trk Co*
        237th Trk Co**
        261st Trk Co
        274th Trk Co
        51st Sup Bn* (horse-drawn vehicles)
20th Fld Road Const Unit*
33d Fld Road Const Unit
16th Rear Med Service Gp:
    105th Rear Hosp
    106th Rear Hosp
    107th Rear Hosp
    121st Rear Hosp**
15th Clearing Gp:
    58th Clearing Plat
    60th Clearing Plat**
    62d Clearing Plat
    68th Clearing Plat
22d Fld W Sup Unit
13th Rear Vet Hosp

Note: 1. * Transferred to 28th Army in January 1944.

      2. ** Transferred to 33d Army in April 1944.

The defense of Burma was divided geographically into two parts: 1) central and northern Burma and 2) the coastal zone along the Indian Ocean. It was believed there would be little connection between the operations in these two geographical areas. The 15th Army was in charge of operations in central and northern Burma. The Burma Area Army, having operational direction of the whole Burma area, would also direct the Burma coastal operations.

On 15 April 1943, 15th Army completed its reorganization and located its headquarters at Maymyo, the center of its assigned defense zone. It was realized that the original three divisions of the Army

16

were not sufficient to cover a defense zone which included all of central and northern Burma with an extremely wide (700 miles) front. To bolster its strength, the 31st Division was incorporated into the 15th Army on 10 May 1943 and on 17 June of the same year, the 15th Division (commanded by Lt. Gen. Masabumi Yamanouchi) was transferred from the command of the China Expeditionary Army at Nanking and incorporated into the 15th Army.

The 31st Division had completed the major portion of its organization by the end of May 1943, but some elements were still in French Indo-China and Malaya. The commander of the 15th Army called for the advance of the 31st Division, or at least the division staff, to Burma to prepare for future operations. Accordingly, 31st Division headquarters advanced to Pegu early in July.

The 15th Army was driven by necessity to give up its original defense plan and advance the first defense line from the Zibyu Range west to the Chindwin River. Realizing that the Chindwin River would not serve as a major obstacle during the dry season the Army staff then considered it necessary to advance the first defense line further west to the steep Arakan Range and to launch an offensive into India, the source of enemy operations. The Army commander believed that preparations for an invasion of India could be conducted without difficulty because there still remained considerable time before the next dry season. He believed that a bold strike at Assam would be best, as such an operation would deal a severe blow to the British by destroying their counteroffensive bases in India and would ultimately result in fomenting the struggle for Indian Independence.

In April 1943, the 15th Army commander suggested to the Area Army commander that an attack be launched along the lines of the plan for Operation No. 21.

Maj. Gen. Obata, Chief of Staff of the 15th Army, declined to support the 15th Army commander, being of the opinion that the execution of the proposed offensive would be difficult in view of the low combat strength of the Army and the lack of rear echelon preparations.

Operations and Reconnaissance West of the Chindwin River

With the completion of the reorganization of 15th Army Headquarters and its move to Maymyo on 15 April 1943, the Army took further measures to drive the remnants of the Wingate Brigade beyond the Chindwin River. The Army commander realized the necessity of determining the actual enemy situation and the nature of the terrain in that area. Accordingly, he ordered two units, each of which had an infantry battalion of the 18th Division as a nucleus, to pursue the enemy forces along the Indaw-Pinbon-Homalin Road and the Wuntho-Pinlebu-Paungbyin Road toward the Chindwin River. In addition the Army ordered a part of the 33d Division to pursue the enemy from Mawlaik to Pantha. According to reports from the units, the roads were in such condition that only elephants could get through and there was little local food available.

The 15th Army commander desiring to advance the front line to the Chindwin River as early as possible to expedite preparations for the invasion of Manipur and Assam, dispatched several staff officers to the Zibyu Range and the basin of the Chindwin River to make a detailed survey of the terrain. The survey was completed by the end of May 1943 and the following information was obtained:

    1. The area permits operation of pack horse units.

    2. The Pinbon-Homalin Road can be easily converted to a dry season motor road. The reconstruction of the Pinlebu-Paungbyin Road is difficult but not impossible.

    3. During the dry season, the Chindwin River can be easily crossed by employing light river crossing materials obtainable locally.

    4. The inhabitants of the Chindwin River basin are the Shans, who are friendly toward the Japanese Army.

    5. The roads running along the banks of the Chindwin River are poor, and it is difficult to move from Homalin to Kalewa except by water transport.

    6. The basin of the Chindwin River, especially the Homalin and Paungbyin sectors, is comparatively densely populated (population estimated at about 100,000). Local acquisition of auxiliary provisions sufficient for five to six battalions is possible.

    7. A part of the enemy has already advanced to the western bank of the Chindwin River. Enemy

> reconnaissance of the eastern bank is becoming more active and repair work on the Tamu-Sittaung Road is under way.

During April and May the enemy in the Chin Hills intensified its activities against front line key positions of the 33d Division near Kalemyo. In order to check the movements of the enemy, elements of the Division captured Third Stockade, about 11 miles west of Kalemyo and at the end of May the Division advanced its defense line to the Chin Hills. As a result, the Division succeeded in dominating the southern part of the Kabaw Valley.

The Army commander believed now that if a defense line south of Homalin were established on the plateau between the Chindwin and the Yu Rivers, the line would be stronger than the defenses along the Chindwin. This line would take advantage of the steep terrain to allow a reduction in the defense force and would also permit reconnaissance and preparations for future offensive operations west of the Chindwin River.

General Mutaguchi, 15th Army Commander, had not abandoned his plan to invade eastern India, however, the Army did not have authority to operate across the Burma-India border. He determined, therefore, to carry out the operation of re-establishing the line as the initial step toward the eventual execution of his plan for the invasion of eastern India. The movement to the west was termed the "Bu" Operation.

Planning for Operation "Bu"

Operation "Bu" would be a surprise attack scheduled for late May 1943 when the rainy season would hinder enemy countermoves. Two powerful elements of the 18th Division would occupy positions west of Homalin and Sittaung, and a part of the 33d Division would occupy a line from Mawlaik west to Yazagyo. For the crossing of the Chindwin River, all river crossing materials of the Army were to be reserved for use by the 18th Division. In addition, local boats would be collected and assigned for the Division's use.

The greatest difficulty to be encountered in the execution of this operation was that, since repairs on the Zibyu Mountain Range road were still incomplete, during the coming rainy season supply for the forces engaged in the operation might be interrupted. Because of probable supply difficulties and the fact that the troops were exhausted due to continuous operations, the 18th Division commander felt that the execution of this operation would be extremely difficult. Consequently, the Army commander decided to concentrate upon the completion of the operational road in the Zibyu Range and to discontinue the "Bu" Operation temporarily. His decision may have been influenced by Maj. Gen. Obata, Chief of Staff, 15th Army, who believed that it would be difficult to complete the operation in the short time estimated by the Army commander. He was afraid that, if the operation should extend over a long period, the transfer of the main strength of the 18th Division to the Hukawng sector would be delayed and that the rainy season would begin with the "Bu" Operation only half finished. Although, he wished to urge the Army commander to reconsider his plans, he thought that it would be more effective to express his opinion to the Army commander through Lt. Gen. Tanaka, 18th Division commander, rather than directly. General Tanaka transmitted General Obata's opinion to the Army commander, who stated that he thought the staff officer's actions on the matter were a violation of Army command channels. The Army commander appreciated the opinion of his chief of staff, but was dissatisfied with his methods and urged his replacement from the standpoint of closer military control. On 15 May, Maj. Gen. Momoyo Kunomura was appointed chief of staff, replacing Maj. Gen. Obata. This strengthened the Army commander's position for the invasion of India.

Re-disposition of 33d Division

Owing to the exigencies of the Akyab and Wingate Operations few 33d Division units were allowed the periods of rest or training that had been expected. After the pursuit of Wingate, the division was forced to secure the strategic area along the Chindwin River and emphasis was placed on positive operations. The progress of the division units up to the end of the rainy season are summarized as follows:

Hq, 33d Division:
: Moved from Yenanggaung to Kalaw on 17 February, advanced to Thetkegyin in early October.

Hq, 33d Infantry Group:
: Advanced from Monywa to Kalewa in May, moved back again to Monywa in June, advanced to Paluzawa 18 miles north of Kalewa on 20 September.

213th Infantry Regiment:
: After the 1st Akyab Operation, the Regimental Headquarters and 2d Battalion moved to Taunggyi in July, then to Yazagyo in October. The balance of the regiment remained in the Akyab area until December, when the 3d Battalion moved to Yazagyo.

214th Infantry Regiment:
: The 1st Battalion was disposed throughout the Pakokku and Gangaw areas. The other units moved to Taunggyi in January, returning to Pakokku in September. The entire regiment advanced to Kalemyo in October.

215th Infantry Regiment:
: The 3d Battalion remained in Kalewa and vicinity. Other units moved to Hsamonghkam east of Kalaw in January, but soon after were dispatched to mop-up the Wingate Brigade. Thereafter the regiment was disposed in the area of Mawlaik, Indainggyi and Kalewa.

33d Mountain Artillery Regiment:

: The 1st Battalion remained at Myingyan, until attached to 214th Regiment in September. The 2d Battalion began to move from Akyab to Yazagyo in October. The 3d Battalion, at Kalewa, was attached to 215th Regiment in September. The other units at Meiktila advanced to Kalewa in October.

33d Engineer Regiment:
: The 2d Company was at Akyab. The main body was engaged in road-construction.

3d Heavy Field Artillery Regiment (less 2d Battalion and half of the Regimental Ammunition Train):
> Moved from Meiktila to the sector south of Yazagyo in October.

18th Heavy Field Artillery Regiment:
> The 1st Battalion was placed at Mutaik 10 miles southeast of Kalewa in March. The remainder of the regiment was stationed at Yenangyaung in March, remaining there until October when the 2d Battalion advanced to the sector south of Yazagyo and the Regimental Headquarters to Mutaik.

Organization of the 31st Division

The organization of the 31st Division was ordered on 22 March 1943. The infantry group of the Division was composed of the 25th Independent Brigade (58th and 138th Infantry Regiments), from Malaya, and the 124th Infantry Regiment, transferred from the Guadalcanal area. The Mountain Artillery Regiment and the Engineer Regiment were organized with personnel drawn from units in central and northern China, respectively. The units organized in areas other than the southern area landed at Saigon and Singapore and were transported to Bangkok by sea and rail. The main force advanced to Pegu on foot and from there proceeded by rail to the prearranged area of disposition, on the right bank of the Irrawaddy River, north of Mandalay. Certain elements of the Division, including the Mountain Artillery Regiment, the Field Hospital and the Field Medical Unit, were transported by boat from Penang to Rangoon to accelerate the assembling of the Division but it was close to September 1943 before the full strength arrived in the vicinities of Indaw, Wuntho, Pinlebu and Pinbon.

One battalion each from the 58th and 138th Regiments had reached the area west of the Zibyu Mountain Range. Their movement was beset by great difficulties, due to the fact that it was the closing period of the rainy season, most of the bridges of the Indaw-Pinbon road had been swept away and the roads running through the Zibyu Range were muddy and hard to traverse. Making matters more difficult, current crops in the Homalin-Paungbyin area were so poor that there were only enough provisions procurable locally to support one infantry battalion.

To provide logistic support for future operations, the 31st Division constructed field depots at Pinlebu and Pinbon. Rafts were built by local inhabitants in order to permit utilization of the branch waterways of the Chindwin River to transport to Homalin provisions accumulated at Pinbon. The front line units depended mostly on manpower to effect their own supply over the Zibyu Mountain paths.

Troop disposition of the 31st Division in late November 1943 was as follows:

        Division Headquarters   )
)...Naungkan
        Infantry Group Headquarters   )

        138th Infantry Regiment
            (less 3d Battalion) ....Panghkok, 20 miles
                                       SE of Homalin

    3d Battalion .... Tonmalaw, 14 miles
                                  SW of Tamanthi

58th Infantry Regiment
   (less 2d and 3d Battalion)..Wayongon

    2d Battalion.......... Magyobyit, 10 miles
                                  NE of Pinlebu

    3d Battalion.......... Ontha, 7 miles S of
                                  Paungbyin

124th Infantry Regiment.... Banmauk

31st Mountain Artillery
   Regiment (less 2d Battalion).. Mansi

    2d Battalion.......... Pinlebu

31st Engineer Regiment .... Hwemaukkan, 7 miles
                                  NW of Pinbon

31st Supply Regiment ...... Indaw

CHAPTER 2

PLANS AND PREPARATIONS FOR THE INVASION OF EASTERN INDIA

The first Wingate Operation had proved that the defenses east of the Chindwin River could be easily pierced and, after receiving information of Allied preparations for an offensive, General Mutaguchi, 15th Army commander, keenly felt the necessity of taking positive action to insure the defense of Burma. In late April 1943, upon receipt of General Mutaguchi's suggestion of an offensive beyond the Chindwin River, General Kawabe, Burma Area Army commander, directed the 15th Army to make immediate plans for such an offensive. On 5 May 1943, General Kawabe reported to the Southern Army on the necessity of an offensive to secure the defense of Burma. The Southern Army and the Burma Area Army agreed to hold a conference at Rangoon in mid-June to study the grand strategy for the defense of Burma.

Preliminary Planning for Operations in India

In early June, 15th Army Headquarters conducted a study of the eastern India invasion operations. The operation plans studied were similar to those for Operation No. 21, but with the 31st Division now under the command of the Army, the plan generally stood as follows:

In the first phase of the operation (border engagement), the Army would direct its major thrust with the main force of the 33d and the 31st Divisions from the Kabaw Valley toward the sector along the road connecting Sittaung, Palel, and Imphal, and after smashing the enemy opposition in this sector would launch a strong coordinated attack upon Imphal.

The main force of the 18th Division would advance from the Hukawng area and occupy the sector around Tinsukia.

After the enemy on the Imphal Plain had been destroyed, the 31st Division would continue to pursue the enemy along the Imphal-Kohima Road and advance as far as the end of Priphema Hill, 24 miles east of Dimapur. Meanwhile, the 33d Division would mop up the enemy remaining on the Imphal Plain and one element would occupy Silchar, covering the left flank of the Army.

Subsequently the 18th Division would assemble in the vicinity of Golaghat and the 31st and 33d Divisions would assemble in the areas north and south of Dimapur to prepare for the second phase of the operation.

In the second phase of the Operation (main engagement), the Army would conduct a final battle in the area west of Golaghat with the enemy main force which could logically be expected to be assembled in eastern India at the end of the first phase of the operation.

Although this operational plan underwent various alternations in respect to employment of forces as a result of repeated map studies and war games, the basic idea remained unchanged. The Army commander laid special emphasis on the necessity of counteracting the restrictions placed on logistics due to the difficult terrain by capturing not only enemy transport facilities but also enemy weapons and ammunition.

Map Maneuver at Rangoon

The Burma Area Army planned and conducted a map maneuver at Rangoon on 24 - 27 June 1943. The Army commander and staff officers of the 15th Army, the chiefs of staff and operations staff officers of all divisions under the Area Army participated. The 5th Air Division also participated in the maneuver as a supporting unit. Officers of the Southern Army and Imperial General Headquarters acted as observers while the 15th Army acted as the blocking force.

The objective of the maneuver was the establishment of the Army line of defense. The maneuver plan was based on the assumption that after a meeting engagement with the advance elements of the enemy at Kabaw Valley, the 15th Army would repulse and pursue the enemy toward Imphal, and then wage a decisive battle on the Imphal Plain against the main force of the enemy. The 31st Division would deploy in the area north of Homalin and advance to Kohima; the 15th Division would deploy in the area east of Thaungdut and Paungbyin and attack Imphal from the north; the 33d Division would deploy in the sector between Fort White and Kalewa and attack Imphal from the south.

In view of the strength and logistical capabilities of the force to be used in the offensive, the operational theater was limited to the Imphal Plain and its immediate vicinity. The conference concluded that Imphal should be taken with a coordinated series of sudden attacks and the defensive line would then be established along the mountain range to the west of the Imphal Plain.

General Mutaguchi was not satisfied with the limited objectives established at the conference. He desired to drive further into India, generally following the objectives of the discarded Operation No. 21. Although his conception of the Imphal Operation was rejected in the conference, it appeared that he had not entirely dispaired of carrying out his original plan, as his troop disposition was the same as it had been when the 15th Army was planning to employ two divisions in the sector north of Imphal.

After Generals Kawabe and Mutaguchi left the conference hall, reviews of the results of the map maneuver were given by Lt. Gen. Naka, Chief of Staff, Burma Area Army, and Maj. Gen. Inada, Vice-Chief of Staff, Southern Army. Inada stated that if the presently planned operation would result in the involvement of the 15th Army in the sectors north of Imphal, the plan would not be approved by the Southern Army. It was clear that his attitude was dictated by the desire to prevent the aggressive 15th Army commander from risking an offensive which might well prove to be strategically and tactically unsound. Strangely, Inada's opinion was not reported to Mutaguchi and troop disposition for the Imphal Operation was made more in accordance with the latter's ideas than with those of the Area Army and the Southern Army.

After the map maneuver was concluded several staff officers were killed on the way back in an air accident that greatly affected the subsequent operations. Among those killed were: Col. Yokoyama, Chief of Staff, 18th Division; Lt. Col. Oi, Staff officer, 18th Division, Col. Kurokawa, Chief of Staff, 56th Division; Lt. Col. Hakamada, staff officer, 56th Division; and Major Mase, staff officer, 15th Division.

Although General Tojo had long contemplated the possibility of striking at British India politically, the operational planners were hesitant to invade India lest Japan's combat potentiality be overtaxed. After the map maneuvers at Rangoon, however, Imperial Army General Headquarters gradually turned toward a more positive policy.

Early in July, the Southern Army submitted a formal suggestion to Tokyo on the necessity of taking the offensive in Burma, and requested reinforcement by the 2d and 54th Divisions, 24th Mixed Brigade, and a proportionate strength of logistical units, as well as supplies of ammunition for four divisions for three months and parts for 1,000 motor vehicles.

In early August, Imperial General Headquarters issued the order to prepare for the Imphal Operation but at that time it was still not certain that the Imphal Operation would actually be carried out.

Development of Imphal Operation Plans

The Burma Area Army basic plan of the eastern India invasion operations was to bolster the defense of Burma by destroying the enemy's strong counterattacking points and advancing the line of defense to the Arakan Mountain Range. In connection with this new line of defense, two plans were conceived by the Area Army. The first, which reflected the views of officers in charge of logistics, would establish the line of defense on the west side of the Kabaw Valley or along the mountain range on the east side of the valley, destroying the enemy's advance bases in the vicinity of Tamu. The second plan would advance the line of defense to the mountain range on the west side of the Imphal Plain, destroying the enemy's counterattacking bases at Imphal. The conclusion reached at the Rangoon meeting was that it would be difficult to establish a defense line at the Kabaw Valley, ignoring the enemy's main strength at Imphal, and the second plan was favored. The 15th Army now supported the execution of a drastic policy, both political and military, against India to bring about a decisive result in the political trend within India and the severance of air transportation between India and China.

The two plans, which reflected the views of the Area Army staff, would limit the operation to the Imphal Plain. A third plan, supported by the 15th Army commander, would gradually extend the operation to the line connecting the Dimapur and Shillong Plains and the

Brahmaputra River. This plan called for an ultimate invasion of eastern India by an advance on Shillong Hill and then an expansion of the front to the Brahmaputra River with a concurrent auxiliary operation from the Chittagong area. The 15th Army plan would reserve as a second line group three to four divisions, besides the three divisions earmarked for the Imphal Operations. With the development of the Manipur occupation, the second line group would be advanced by leapfrog tactics while the group operating in the Hukawng Valley would advance to Sibsagar by way of Ledo. This third plan was almost a replica of the plan for Operation No. 21, to which the Area Army officers and higher authorities had been very cold.

A close personal relationship had existed between Kawabe and Mutaguchi for many years. Kawabe admired Mutaguchi's aggressive spirit and Mutaguchi was devoted to his superior officer. In spite of this, General Kawabe also took a stand against the plan so strongly advanced by General Mutaguchi.

A logistical plan, to support the favored operation against Imphal, was formulated by Area Army Headquarters and 15th Army Headquarters to establish a supply line for each of three operational groups during the early phase of the operation and a main supply line, using the road connecting Kalewa, Tamu, and Imphal, after the occupation of Imphal. (Map No. 3).

MAP NO. 3

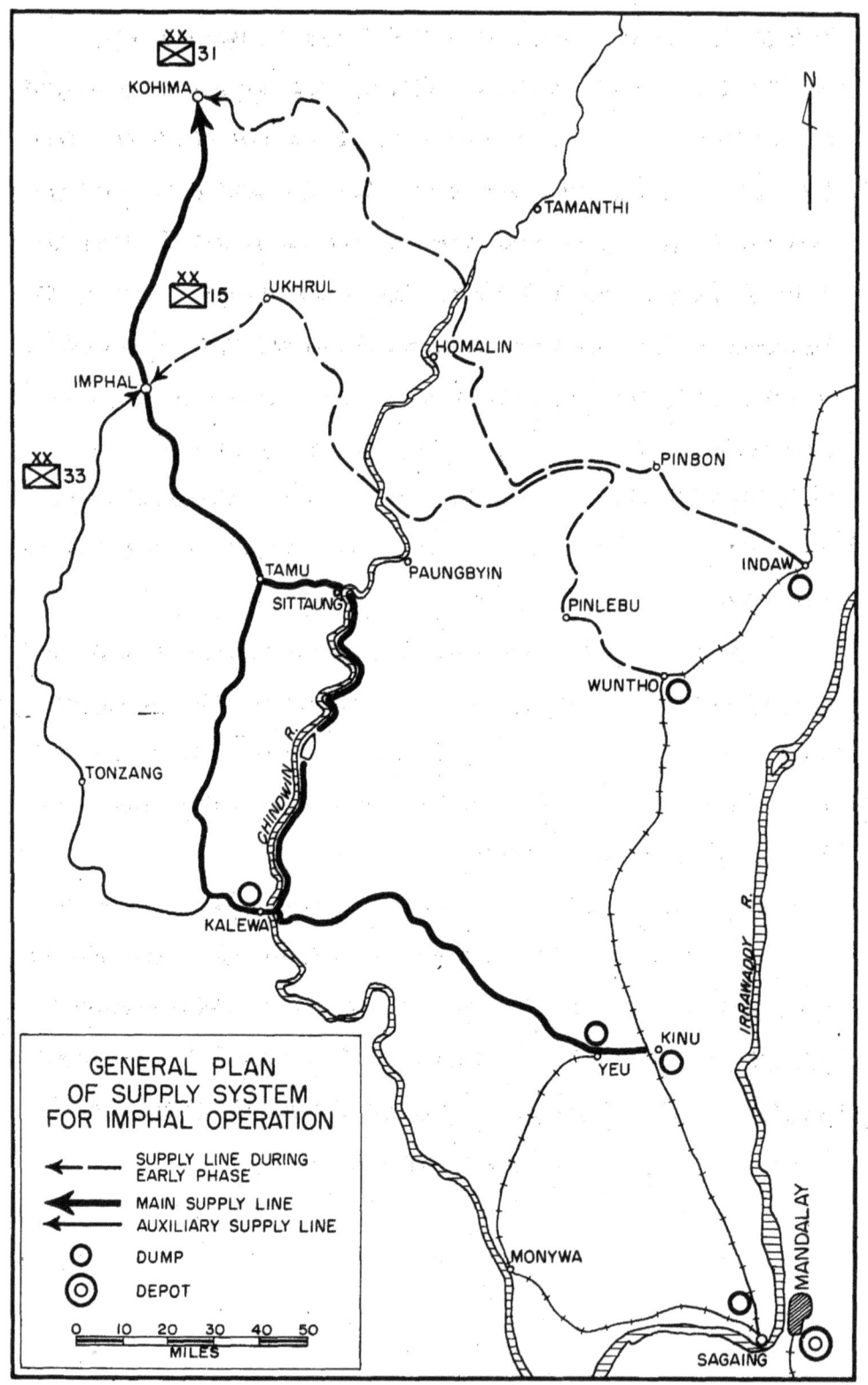

Policy of Imperial General Headquarters Toward India

The Indian National Army (INA), which came into existence during the Malaya Operations in December 1941, grew so rapidly after the fall of Singapore that, on 22 August 1942, Imperial General Headquarters began to conduct a definite policy toward India, based upon the INA and the Indian Independence League. The main objective of the policy was to help to intensify the anti-British and independence movements thereby making it impossible for Britain to exploit India in the battle against Japan.

Subhas Chandra Bose, who was conducting the independence movement from Berlin, was invited to eastern Asia by the Japanese Government. In May 1943, he travelled incognito to Penang and then to Tokyo. He conferred with Japanese government authorities in Tokyo and it was decided to foster an intensive anti-British independence movement in India. On 1 July, Bose went to Singapore and established the Provisional Government of Free India, whose leadership he took while also assuming the post of Commander-in-Chief of the INA. Encouraged by the appearance of Chandra Bose, the India independence movement grew very strong in eastern Asia and the Thai and Burmese Governments began actively supporting the movement. There were approximately 2,000,000 Indian nationals living in Burma and 100,000 in Thai who exerted a strong influence on the Provisional Government of Free India.

In view of the political situation within and without India, Bose strongly desired a Japanese Army invasion of India which would to be executed with the support of the INA and he presented his opinion concerning this matter to the Japanese authorities. The development of Japanese political policy toward India exerted influence on both Imperial General Headquarters and the operational armies concerning grand strategy in Burma operations.

Enemy Situation in September 1943

The situation of the enemy forces in August 1943 was as follows:

1. In the Akyab sector the enemy had disposed, in depth, the British-Indian 5th and 7th Divisions on the Buthidaung-Maungdaw front with two or three additional divisions behind them, and there were obvious signs of preparations for an offensive in the near future.

2. In the province of Assam, Imphal and its vicinity was the base of enemy operations and the British-Indian 17th, 20th and 23d Divisions as well as one other division had been advancing to this sector. The enemy was reconstructing the Imphal-Palel-Tamu Road and the Imphal-Churachandpur-Tiddim Road into motor vehicle roads.

3. In the Hukawng Valley the New 1st Army of the Chungking Army and a U.S. Brigade commanded by Gen. Joseph E. Stilwell had been stationed near Ledo. The real power of the New 1st Army was far superior to that of the former Chinese Army in respect to organization, equipment and training. Here, too, were seen indications of an offensive which might be expected before long.

4. In the Yunnan area approximately ten divisions of the Yunnan Expeditionary Army (Chinese) had taken positions on the east bank of the Salween River west of Tali. It was estimated that the enemy preparations for operations in this area were slower than those in other areas and that the troops stationed there lacked the power to launch an independent counterattack but were ready to stage an offensive in cooperation with a counteroffensive from the eastern India area.

Final Imphal Operation Planning

Southern Army Order for Preparations

On 7 August, the Southern Army issued the following order to the Burma Area Army:

    1. The Burma Area Army will complete preparations for a counteroffensive (hereafter to be called the U-Go Operation) to offset a possible large scale enemy offensive, but will not prepare for Operations No. 21, No. 22 and No. 32.

    2. Standard operational control for the U-Go Operation:

        a. The Burma Area Army will take the offensive in the direction of Imphal, with the main force disposed on the west side of the Chindwin River, will defeat the enemy in the vicinity of the border area, destroy the enemy in the Imphal area, and will establish a strong defense in the vicinity. Meanwhile, the armies on the other fronts will take measures to delay and pin down the enemy. It is expected that this operation will commence no sooner than the early part of 1944.
        Approximately seven divisions will be available for operations in Burma.
        b. If the enemy launches a major offensive prior to completion of our preparations, the Burma Area Army will check and

destroy the enemy in areas as close to our bases as possible and will pursue them to Imphal.

c. The time for launching the offensive is subject to approval by the Southern Army Headquarters.

d. Depending upon the situation, the Burma Area Army will merely advance its defensive zone to an advantageous line.

Burma Area Army Strategic Plan

The strategy of the Burma Area Army for the Imphal Operation based on the enemy situation and the Southern Army order was established in early August 1943 and the order regarding preparations for the operation was issued on 12 August:

1. The 15th Army will advance to Imphal before enemy preparations for a counteroffensive could be completed. After crushing the enemy at Imphal, our forces will seize the Arakan Mountain Range and establish the defense line there. This move will serve to break the western wing of the enemy's pincer movement against Burma from India and China, and establish a base from which further action, both political and operational, can be exploited.

2. An offensive by the 55th Division will be started against the Akyab area two or three weeks before the commencement of the Imphal Operation to contain the enemy in that area. The 18th Division will be responsible for the Hukawng Valley and will check the enemy in the sector beyond Kamaing during the operation.

3. The 56th Division will make efforts to defend against the Yunnan force on the line of the Salween River, and will hold at any costs the Pingka-Lameng-Tengchung sector during the operations.

4. Upon the occupation of Imphal, the provisional government of Free India will be established there in order to accelerate the political campaign in India.

15th Army Tactical Plan

The 15th Army held a conference at Maymyo on 25 - 26 August to brief the division commanders on the tactical plan of the U-Go Operation and issue preparation orders. Lt. Gen. Naka, Chief of Staff of the Burma Area Army attended.

The 15th Army tactical plan for the Imphal Operation proposed a prior operation on the Salween River front to destroy the counter-offensive bases of the Chungking Army on the west bank of the river, and to seize the river crossing points. This surprise attack along the river between Tengchung and Hpimaw would begin about the middle of October 1943. The 56th Division and a powerful element of the 18th Division would take part in the attack.

On the Hukawng Valley front, the main body of the 18th Division would establish its base of operations near Mogaung and hold off a possible enemy attack from Ledo north of Kamaing. After the conclusion of the Salween River operation, units of the 18th Division participating in that operation would move to the Hukawng front. Elements of the 18th Division would hold the strategic points around Myitkyina and guard the Myitkyina, Sumprabum, Fort Hertz and the Hpimaw-Lukou Road areas.

The 15th Army would commence the Imphal Operation at the end of 1943 or early in 1944, prior to the counterattack by the British-Indian forces. However, if the enemy should start a counteroffensive before the 15th Army attack, the Army would intercept and smash the counteroffensive and immediately advance to occupy Imphal. After the occupation, the Army forces would hold the key line from Kohima to Falam and Haka through the mountain range west of Imphal and the high ground on the west bank of the Manipur River, and would prepare for subsequent operations.

Between late October and mid-November, the 33d Division would capture Fort White, Falam and Haka, key points in the Chin Hills, and would dispose its main force around Kalemyo and an element around Mawlaik. Then the Division would make preparations for an offensive on the line linking Mawlaik, Yazagyo and Fort White. The main body of the 33d Division would operate toward Imphal along the Tiddim-Bishenpur-Imphal Road, while a powerful element would move from the Kabaw Valley along the Tamu-Palel-Imphal Road to cooperate with the main force.

In order to make preparations for the Imphal Operation, the 31st Division would first concentrate its main force in the Indaw-Wuntho-Pinbon-Pinlebu sector and deploy elements at Tamanthi, Homalin and Paungbyin, key points on the east bank of the Chindwin River. The main force would advance to the Chindwin River just before the commencement of the offensive, cross the river at Homalin and points north, advancing toward Kohima via Layshi and Fort Keary. A powerful element of the Division would cross the river in the vicinity of Homalin and strike at Kohima via Ukhrul and Maram. Both forces would occupy Kohima and check the British-Indian Army reinforcements expected from the Assam area. If the situation permitted, one element would move toward Imphal and participate in the operations there.

Simultaneously with its arrival in Burma, the 15th Division would advance to the Wuntho-Pinlebu sector and relieve the 31st Division. The 15th Division would deploy elements in the vicinity of Paungbyin to make preparations for further operations. The main force of the Division would advance to the Chindwin River just before the commencement of the offensive, cross the river between Homalin and Thaungdut, drive to the northwestern sector of Imphal via Humine and Ukhrul and attack Imphal in coordination with the 33d Division.

After the occupation of Imphal the 31st Division and the main force of the 15th Division would occupy the key points around Kohima and the mountain range west of the Imphal Plain, respectively. The 33d Division would occupy the Chin Hills with one regiment and assemble the main force around Kalewa and Kalemyo.

During the attack phase of the Imphal Operation (estimated at three weeks), supply would be carried out by each force independently. Simultaneously with the invasion of Imphal, the Army would utilize the road linking Kalewa, Tamu, Imphal and Kohima for emergency supplies and would subsequently establish that road as the main supply route.

Acceleration of Logistical Preparations

Road maintenance posed an extremely important problem for the planners of the Imphal Operation, as the only engineer strength available for the Army was the 5th Engineer Command consisting of the 4th and 20th Independent Engineer Regiments and the 20th and 33d Field Road Construction Units. The road net as proposed for the Imphal Operation was as shown on Map No. 4.

Road maintenance was conducted to achieve the following objectives:

    1. Roads to advance combat units which were in the rear areas.

    2. Roads to be used as main lines for future maneuver of troops and supply.

    3. Roads to be used for supply immediately after the initiation of the deployment and the offensive.

    4. Roads to be used as main routes after the completion of operations.

Roads in the first category were generally maintained by a provisional road construction unit (consisting of local inhabitants with military personnel as a nucleus). The Kemapyu-Taunggyi-Kalaw Road and the Takaw-Loilem-Hsipaw Road used to expedite the advance of the 15th Division were repaired by this type of unit.

MAP NO. 4

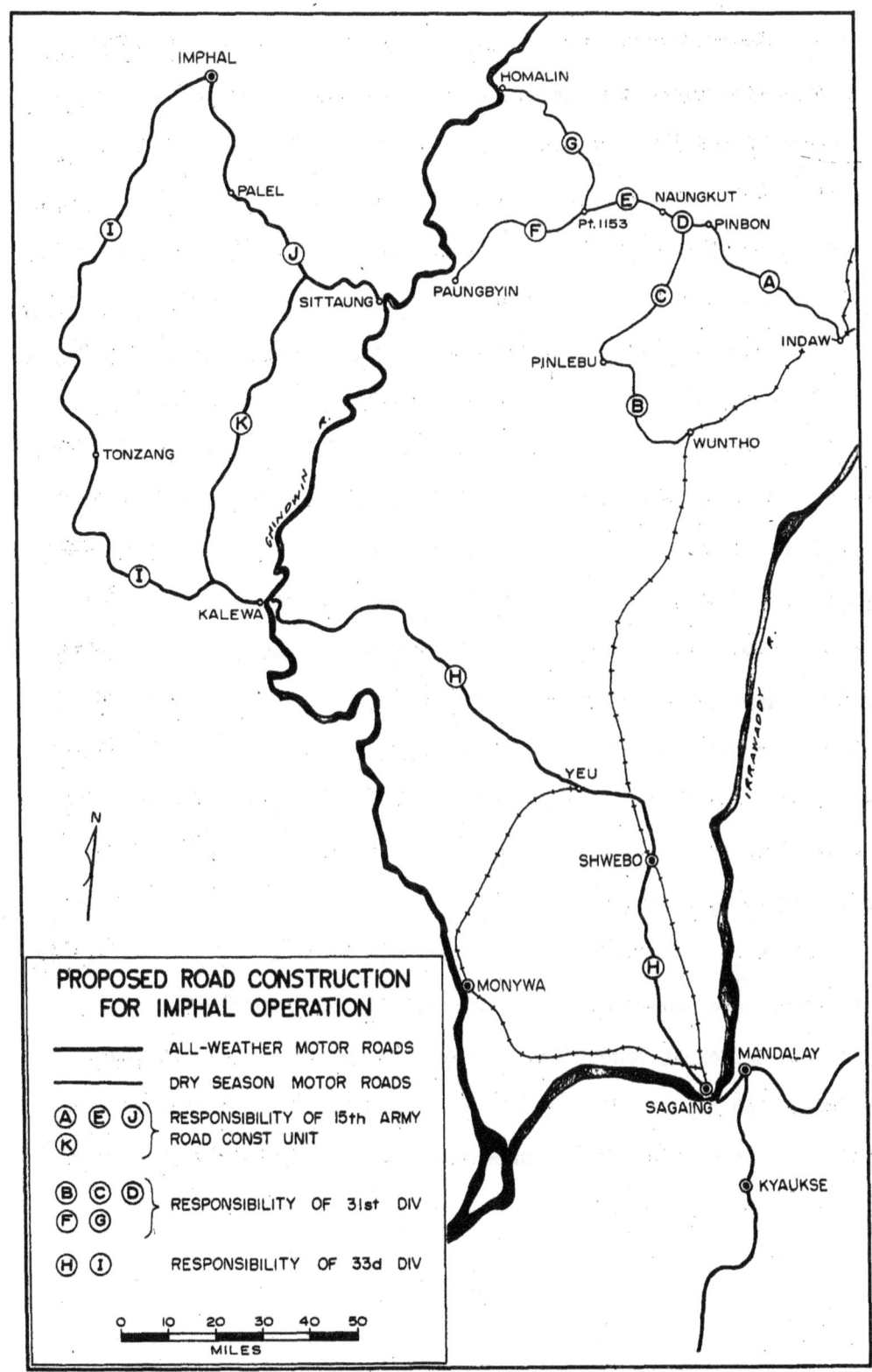

The construction of a motor road to cross the Zibyu Mountain Range was regarded as a prerequisite in making the attack on Imphal. The 15th and 31st Divisions could then be rapidly concentrated on the Chindwin River. An investigation of the roads across the mountains revealed that it was possible to make them into dry season motor roads by repairing bridges in sections A and B and by doing some construction work in sections C, D, F and G. Although the road in section E required considerable construction work and technical skill, it was estimated that it could be opened for traffic in about two months. Based on the conclusion that these roads could be made usable for the deployment of two divisions and their subsequent supply, early in September an order was issued to repair them as dry season motor roads. The Army Road Construction Group (5th Engineer Command Headquarters, 20th Independent Engineer Regiment and the 30th Field Road Construction Unit) was assigned to work on roads in sections A and E while the Engineer Unit of the 31st Division, aided by local inhabitants, was assigned to work on the roads in sections B, C, D, F and G.

Although construction work in section E was extremely difficult, the roads were generally completed by early February 1944.

The principal roads planned for all-weather motor roads for movement and supply north of Mandalay were as follows: Sagaing-Yeu-Kalewa Road; the Kalewa-Tonzang-Imphal Road; and the Sittaung-Palel-Imphal Road.

The 4th Independent Engineer Regiment and the 30th Field Road Construction Unit were to be attached to the 33d Division and charged with construction work on the Sagaing-Shwebo-Kalewa Road. As soon as this road had been generally completed the two attached construction units were to be diverted to aid the road building work across the Zibyu Mountain Range. As soon as the final stage of the offensive was approached, the 33d Division was to be assigned to improve the Kalewa-Tonzang-Imphal Road. The 15th Army Road Building Engineer Group was to be committed to the Sittaung-Imphal road as the offensive progressed, and a powerful element of the 15th Division was to assist after the offensive ended.

Requests were made for the line of communications units to be assigned for the Imphal Operation and tentative approval of a number considerably less than requested was given by the Area Army in August. Final authorizations approved in September were even lower (Chart No. 1).

CHART NO. 1

Logistic Units to Support the Imphal Operation

Type of Unit	Requested by 15th Army (July)	Area Army Estimates (August)	Final Authorization from Area Army (September)
Motor Transport Company	150	90	26
Transport Company	60	40	14
Transport headquarters	3-4	2	2
Logistic sector unit	4	3	1
Rear hospital	8-10	6	3
Rear medical unit	4	3	2
Field road construction unit	4-5	3	2
Independent engineer regiment	5	3	2

Some of the units were to be transferred from Singapore and the South Pacific area. Some were auxiliary troop units to be organized in the various southern territories and consisted mainly of substandard soldiers who were volunteers from the occupied territories. Whether they could efficiently maintain lines of communication was not known. The Army realized that supply would be difficult if the operation covered a long period of time and wished to complete the operation in as short a time as possible. The Army estimated that the divisions could carry on combat operations for a maximum of twenty days with the munitions carried by the divisions. The first stage of the operation was, however, expected to be completed in approximately 20 days.

Supply facilities were established at strategic points throughout the rear areas from which re-supply could be effected (Chart No. 2).

Relations with the Indian National Army

All matters, including both political and military affairs, concerning the INA and the provisional government of Free India in the Burma area were placed under the direct jurisdiction of the Burma Area Army. After the Area Army had conferred and determined the details with the Indian provisional government authorities, those matters to which the Japanese Army had been committed were transmitted

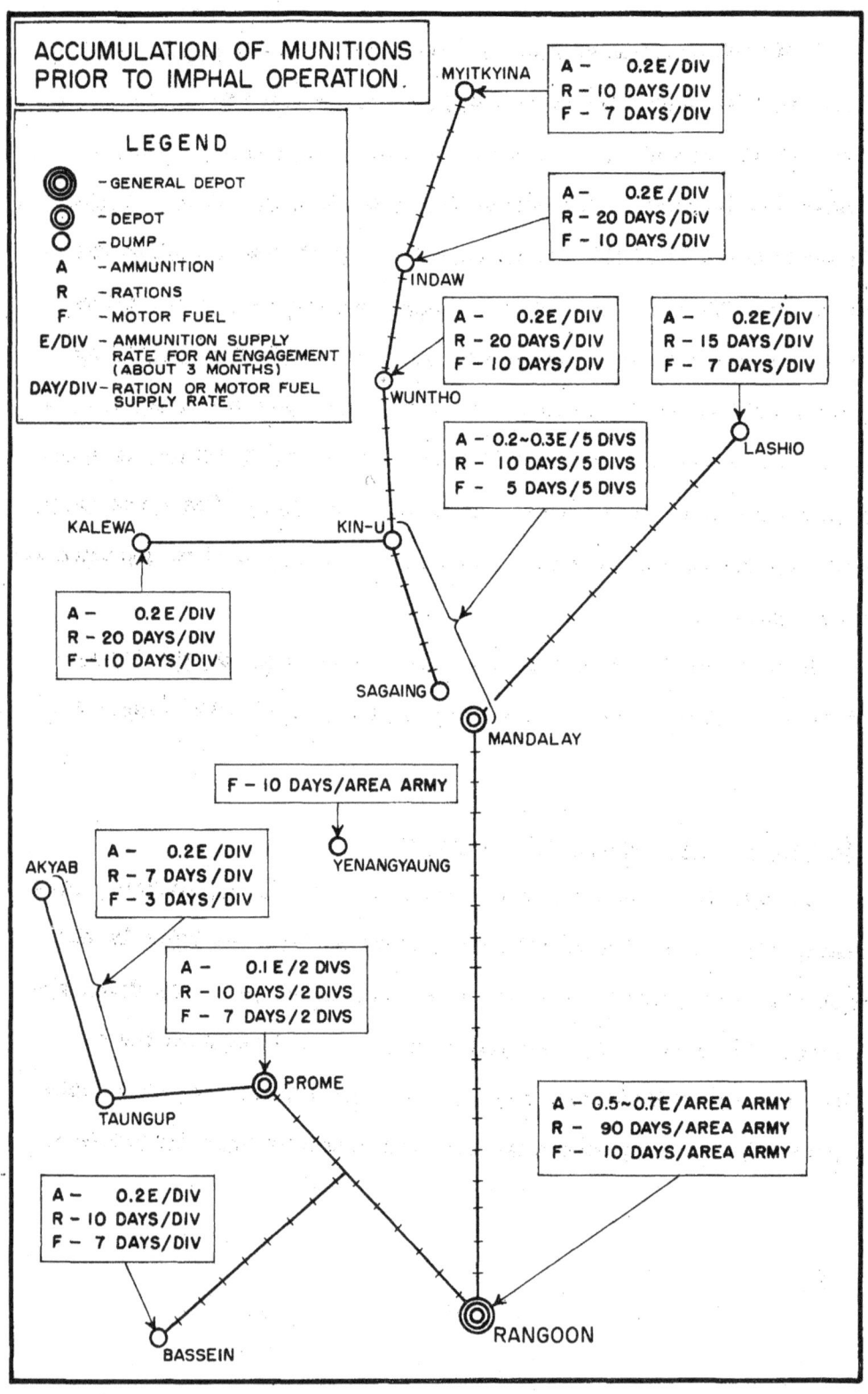

to the Japanese unit concerned by the Area Army.[1] When an element of the INA operated or moved in the zone of operation of a Japanese force, its mission and sector of operation was determined at a liaison officers conference between the Area Army and INA staff officers. Subsequently, the INA unit was placed under the operational command of a Japanese division commander of equivalent or higher rank. The Special Duty, Intelligence, and Replacement Units could be placed under the command of a column commander of a division (usually a regimental commander). Liaison with these units was conducted through the liaison group of the Hikari Agency.

The organization of the INA was as follows:

    1st Division

        Special Duty Unit (to conduct sabotage and guerrilla operations)

        Intelligence Unit (to collect intelligence)

        Replacement Unit (to accept surrenders for the INA)

        Liberated Area Administrative Committee (to take charge of administration of areas occupied by the Japanese Army)

---

1. As a rule, contacts between the Burma Area Army and the INA were made through the "Hikari" Agency, a Japanese-sponsored secret intelligence agency headed by Maj. Gen. Isoda.

Intelligence Collecting Plan

The principal aims of the collection of intelligence by the 15th Army was to acquire knowledge of the enemy's plan of counterattack, topographical data on the Manipur sector and meteorological data concerning the rainy season and its effects.

Intelligence operations were hindered by the vast expanses of jungle and mountains and the fact that the Army was not in contact with the enemy forces, except with those in the Yunnan area. Even after the Army had advanced the first line of defense as far as the Chindwin River, direct reconnaissance was limited by such obstacles as the river and the epidemic-infested areas of the Arakan Range. With regard to the situation of the Chungking Army in the Yunnan area and the U.S. - Chinese forces in the Hukawng area, the collection of intelligence was easier because the Army's Special Intelligence Section could intercept wireless communications and decipher the enemy code.

For collecting intelligence, the Army depended not only upon the units under its command and its supporting agencies, but it also established the following sections:

    Mangshih Special Intelligence Section --
      Deciphering the code of the Chungking Army.

    Maymyo Special Intelligence Section --
      Deciphering the code of the British-Indian forces.

    Monitoring Section --
      Monitoring the broadcasts from Delhi.

Border Secret Operation Team —
Obtaining secret information and working
among the minority races on the border.[2]

Operations in the Salween River Area (Map No. 5)

The Chungking Army on the Salween River front appeared to be making rapid preparations for a counteroffensive with Paoshan as a key position. The enemy force, estimated at about ten divisions, was improving its organization and equipment and showing good results in training, road repair work and the transportation of munitions to the front line. A force, with the Chinese 36th Division as its nucleus, had advanced to the sector north of Tengchung on the west bank of the Salween River.

15th Army Operational Plan

The 15th Army decided to surprise the Chungking Army in Yunnan, destroying its potentiality for a counteroffensive and thereby eliminating this threat of serious interference during the invasion of Assam. In the execution of the operation, Army headquarters adopted a plan restricting the zone of its operations to the west bank of the Salween River which would result in confining the enemy to the east of the river. In addition to the 56th Division, a part of the 18th

---

2. The Area Army recognized the importance of appeasement and utilization of the Burma-India border peoples and after April 1943, had assigned the personnel needed by the Army to be organized as the Border Secret Operation Team.

MAP NO. 5

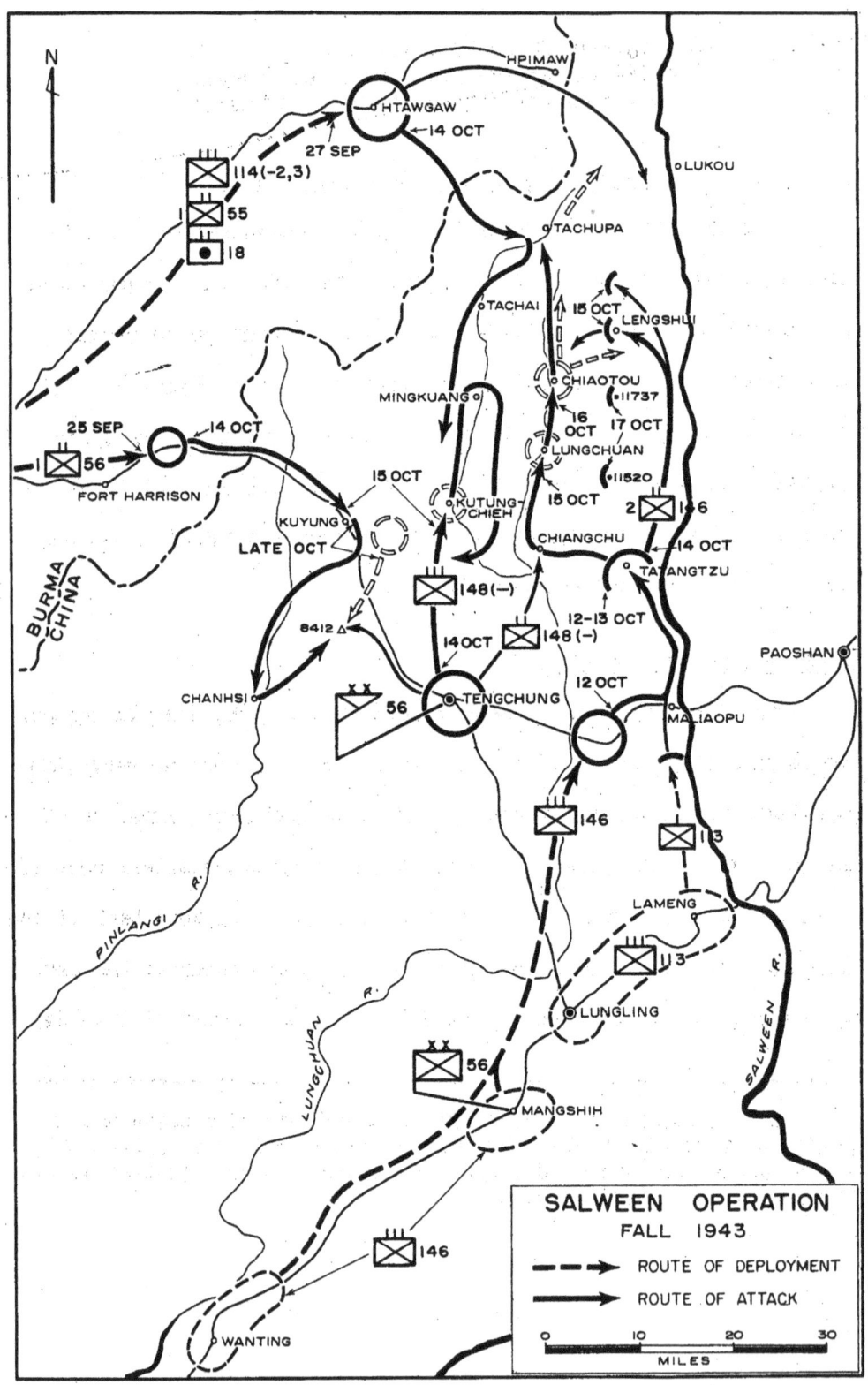

Division (which was supposed to be assigned to operations in the Hukwang area) would have to participate in this operation.

The operational plan entailed having an element of the 56th Division guard against an enemy attack by controlling the Kunlong-Lameng line. The Division's main force, moving north from the Tengchung area, and an element of the 18th Division (three infantry and one artillery battalions) moving east and south from Fort Harrison and Htawgaw, would make their way to Chiaotou and Kutungchieh respectively and launch a converging attack. Special stress was laid on the point that elements of the 56th and 18th Divisions would advance to the Salween River crossing points to check enemy counterattacks from the east bank and cut the enemy's line of retreat on the west bank of the river. The period of operations was scheduled for the last half of October.

Blockade of Salween River Crossings

The troop disposition for this operation was completed in early October. The operation was preceded by the advance of the 146th Infantry Regiment to the phase line at Tatangtzu by 14 October. On the night of 14 October, all units launched their moves simultaneously. The 15th Army advanced its command post to Lashio. On the whole, the operations progressed as expected and the mopping-up operation in Chiaotou and Kutungchieh was completed by the end of October.

MAP NO. 6

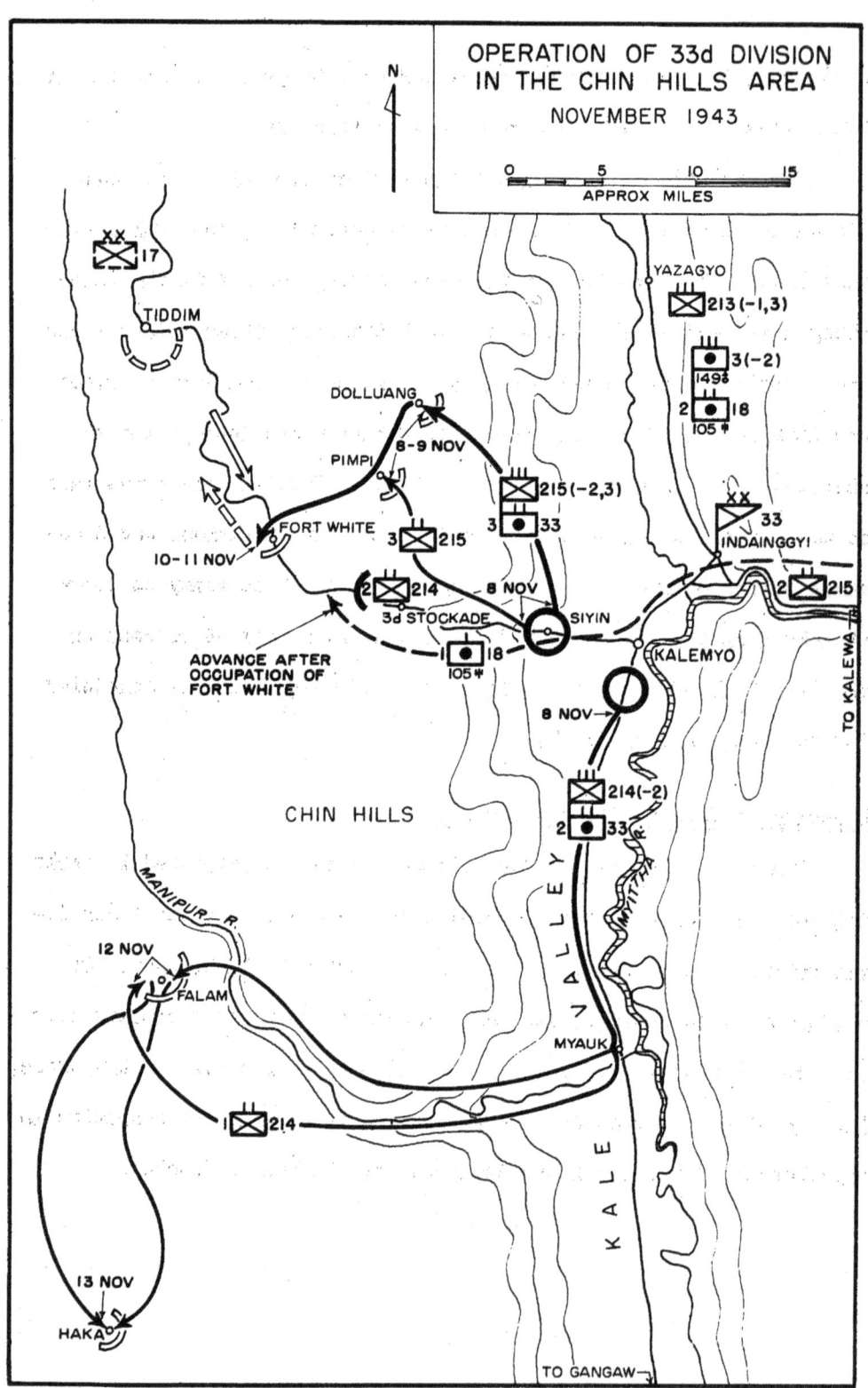

The main strength of the 36th Division of the Chungking Army had been dispersed and, although the Japanese forces failed to completely destroy the division, they succeeded in crushing the key points of the suspected enemy counteroffensive on the western bank of the Salween River and were able to blockade all possible river crossing points.

The Army left the 56th Division to mop-up the remaining enemy and diverted the participating units of the 18th Division to Myitkyina. The objective of this operation was attained with only small losses.

Chin Hills Operations of the 33d Division (Map No. 6)

The enemy in the Chin Hills confronting the 33d Division suddenly came to life just at the close of the rainy season in October 1943. At that time, the 33d Division was stationed along a line connecting Gangaw, Third Stockade and Yazagyo. With Kalewa as the center, it was disposed in a fan-shaped position facing the Chin Hills. The 17th Division of the British-Indian forces, based at Tiddim, with elements confronting the Division in the Tonzang, Yazagyo, Third Stockade and Fort White area, were conducting a thorough reconnaissance of Japanese front line positions which gradually took the form of a reconnaissance in force. A native guerrilla unit, called the "Aijal Brigade", advanced to the Haka and Falam front. Its area of activity extended as far as the Gangaw Valley, where it contacted the Japanese border secret operation team and garrison unit.

As the first important step for the attack on Imphal and in order to shift its disposition for a northward advance the 33d Division was ordered to seize strategic Falam, Haka and Fort White and bring the Chin Hills under control during late October and early November.

The 33d Division commander had misgivings about this operation, believing that it would be more advantageous for the Division to hold its positions on the present defense line and repulse the counterattack of the enemy. He feared that the operation would necessitate committing the main force of the Division to seize the Chin Hills and would disrupt preparations for the forthcoming Imphal Operation. Moreover, it would be difficult to negotiate the muddy mountain trails immediately after the rainy season and to maintain a supply line over 60 miles in length. However, he reluctantly agreed to carry out the operation in compliance with the Army order.

33d Division Operational Plan

The Division commander decided to advance a part of the Division to firmly secure the Mawlaik-Yazagyo area and to take the offensive with the main force to seize Fort White, Haka and Falam on 8 November.

The Division plan was roughly as follows:

    1. The 215th Infantry Regiment (less the 2d Battalion, plus the 3d Battalion of the 33d Mountain Artillery Regiment) will relinquish the defense of Third Stockade to the 2d Battalion, 214th Infantry Regiment, and make attack preparations near Siyin. The Regiment will advance through Dolluang and Pimpi in two columns to occupy the area north of Fort White.

    2. The 214th Infantry Regiment (less the 2d Battalion and plus the 2d Battalion, 33d Mountain Artillery Regiment) will make preparations to attack in area along the Manipur River south of Kalemyo, commence the advance on 8 November, and occupy first Falam and then Haka.

    3. As soon as the 215th Infantry Regiment occupies Fort White, an element of the 18th Heavy Artillery Regiment will take positions near Third Stockade and check the enemy counterattack. The Division command post will be shifted to Indainggyi.

Advancing of Forward Positions

On 8 November the 1st Battalion, 215th Infantry Regiment seized the enemy's forward position in the vicinity of Dolluang and the 3d Battalion took Pimpi. On 10 November, the 1st Battalion advanced to Fort White and struck at the enemy troops there. The enemy made repeated and resolute counterattacks to repulse the enveloping attack. Moreover, the enemy in the vicinity of Kennedy Peak moved under cover of the artillery fire and surrounded the 1st Battalion. On 11 November the enemy retreated and the occupation of the vicinity of Fort White by the 215th Infantry Regiment was accomplished.

MAP NO. 7

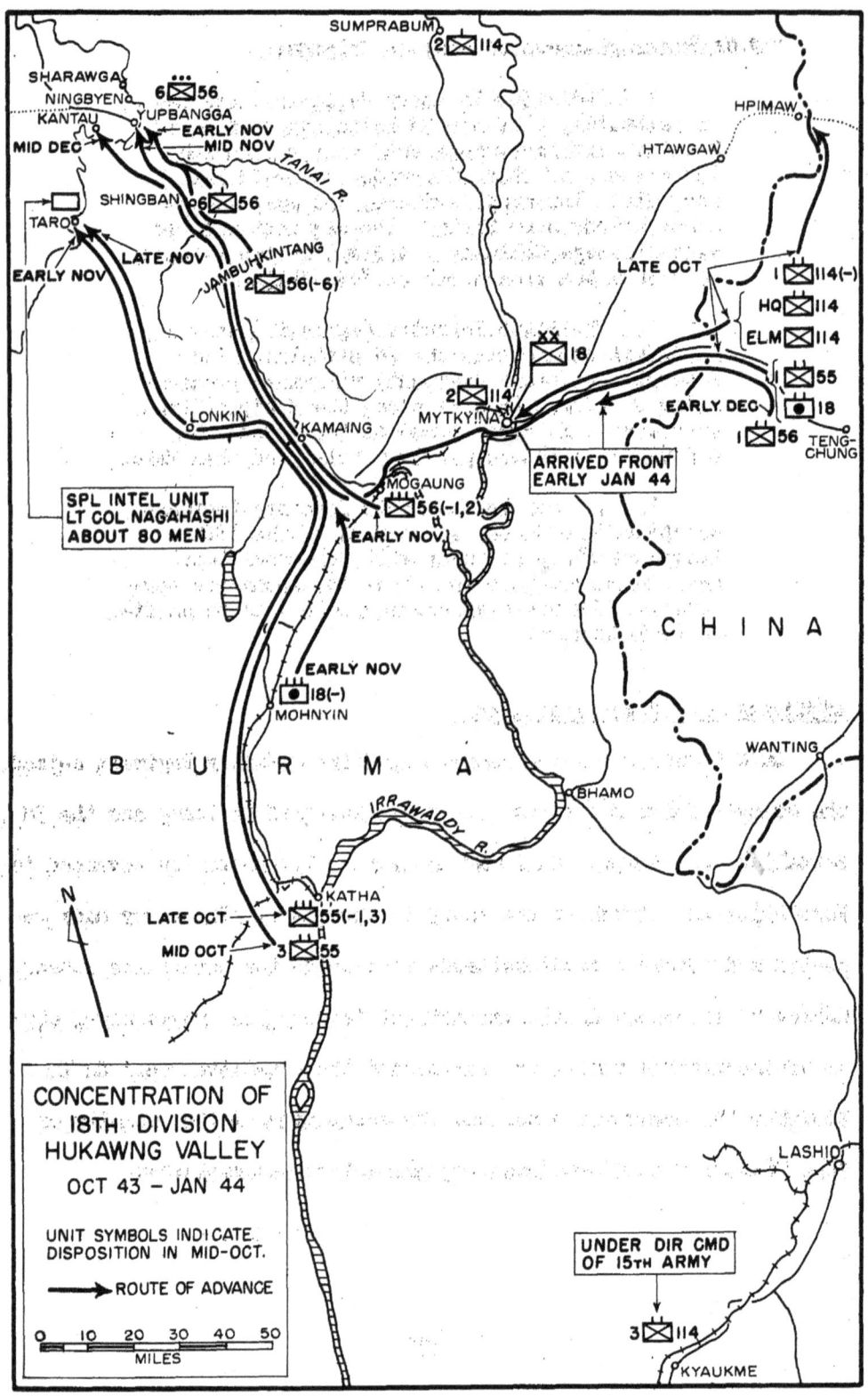

The 1st and the 3d Battalions, of the 214th Infantry Regiment advanced abreast along the Manipur River toward Falam. The advance was over new routes through difficult terrain. On 12 November, the 1st Battalion rushed into Falam from the west after making a detour around the town and the 3d Battalion came in from the east. On 13 November, after assigning a garrison force to guard Falam, the two battalions again advanced by parallel routes to attack Haka. They occupied Haka on the night of 13 November and established defensive positions there.

The 33d Division re-assembled in the vicinity of Third Stockade, Kalemyo and Yazagyo and started preparations for future operations.

Hukawng Operations of the 18th Division (Map No. 7)

When the Yunnan Operation was being brought to a close in late October 1943, the 18th Division Commander at Myitkyina received a report that the Ningbyen Garrison Unit (one platoon of the 2d Battalion, 56th Infantry Regiment) on the Tarung River was involved in an engagement with the 112th Infantry Regiment of the Chinese 38th Division which had come south from Ledo.

As the 18th Division had just begun a new disposition, its main force was still in areas south and east of Kamaing. The following units of the 56th Infantry Regiment were the only forces north of Kamaing:

2d Battalion (less 6th Company)... Jambu Hkintang

6th Company (less one platoon).... Shingban

One platoon, 6th Company .... Sharawga-Ningbyen-Yupbangga Sector

Special Intelligence Party under Lt. Col. Nagahashi (about 80 men) .... Taro

The entire battalion immediately advanced to the Sharawga-Ningbyen-Yupbangga sector to engage the Chinese regiment.

Concentration of Forces

To take advantage of the enemy's movement to the mountainous India-Burma border area, the Division took steps to rapidly concentrate its main force in the Hukawng Valley. Early in November, the Division advanced its headquarters to Kamaing. The enemy which had advanced to Ningbyen and vicinity consisted of a part of the American and Chinese armies which had been assigned to provide cover for the main enemy force advancing through the narrow pass between Ledo and Shingbwiyang. It seemed unlikely that the enemy would be able to immediately send a large force across the India-Burma border, but the Division dispatched the main forces of the 55th and 56th Infantry Regiments to Taro and Yupbangga respectively, with the intention of completely destroying the enemy.

Meanwhile, 2d Battalion, although suffering heavy losses was holding Ningbyen and Sharawga and awaiting the arrival of the 55th and 56th Regiments which were delayed by the rainy season and the muddy roads. With the arrival of the two regiments, in November, the 112th Regiment of the Chungking Army was surrounded and defeated although not completely annihilated.

Beginning in early December the enemy on the west bank of the Tarung River was gradually reinforced and as a consequence the main body of the 55th Regiment was sent to the Tanai River front. (Map No. 8a).

Suspension of the Offensive

To launch an offensive with the main force from Ningbyen toward a defile near Shingbwiyang on the India-Burma border, the Division assembled its forces in the vicinity of Taihpa Ga and commenced preparations for an offensive scheduled for 15 December. In early December, however, the Division chief of staff was summoned to Army headquarters at Maymyo and directed to have the 18th Division stop the present offensive, intercept the enemy in the Maingkwan area and secure the vicinity of Kamaing at all costs. No more troop reinforcements would be sent to the area north of the Tanai River except by specific permission of the Army. Consequently, the Division abandoned plans for an offensive.

The Division commander now thought it necessary to check the enemy and guard against any flanking moves in order to gain sufficient time to complete preparations for the operations to be conducted in the vicinity of Maingkwan.

MAP NO. 8a

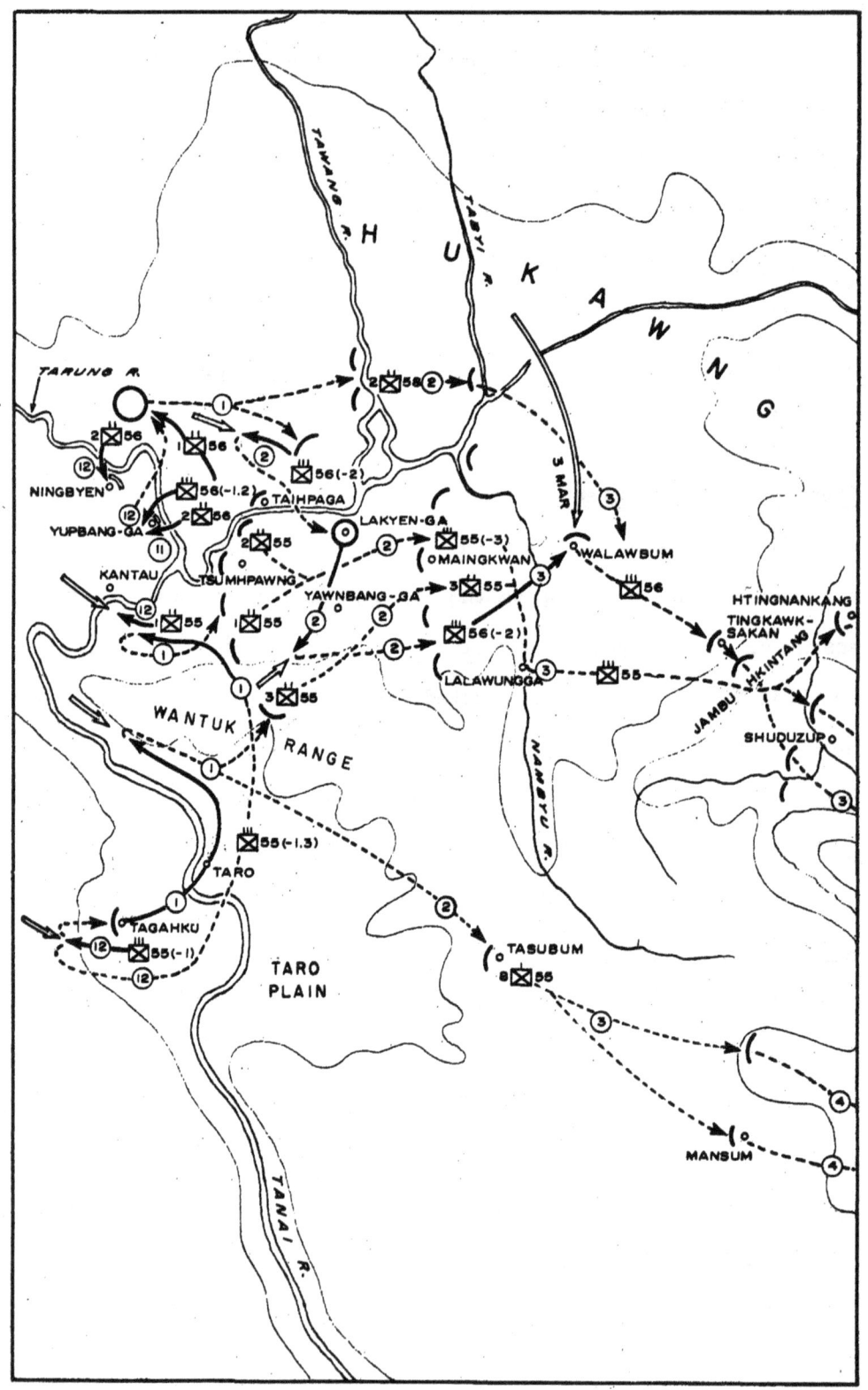

MAP NO. 8 b

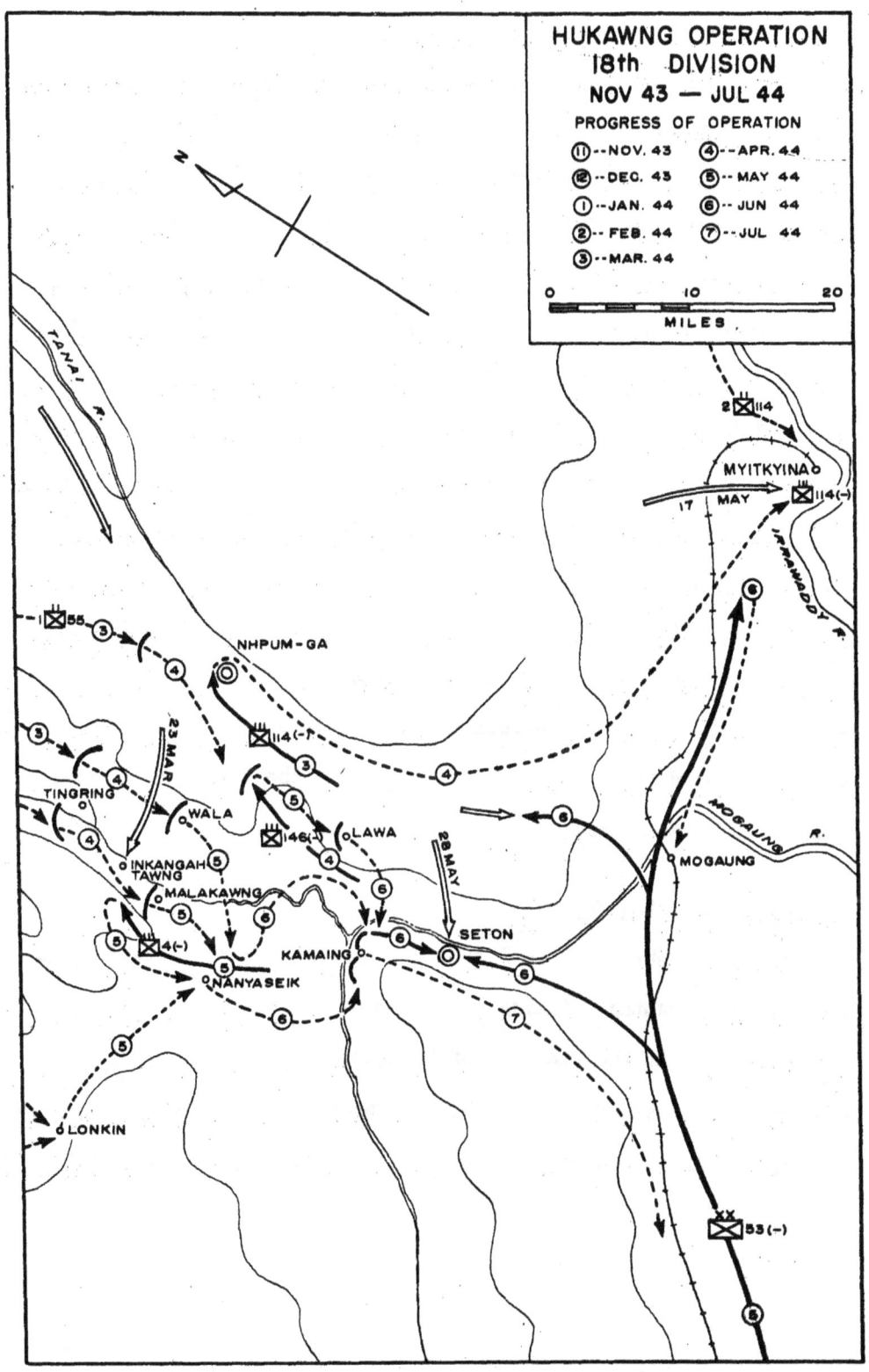

Establishment of the Taihpa Ga Defense

The 55th and 56th Infantry Regiments had suffered heavy losses in the fighting along the Tanai and Tarung Rivers. In January, taking the prevailing circumstances into consideration, the commander of the 18th Division determined that it would be wiser not to fall back to the Maingkwan area immediately. Instead, he decided to establish an active defense along a line running east and west through Taihpa Ga, utilizing the natural barrier provided by the Tanai River. The enemy made an enveloping movement eastward on the Division's right flank with a powerful element and, at the same time, attempted to break through the left flank by penetrating the Wantuk Mountain Range. The fiercest engagement was fought on the front of the 55th Infantry Regiment in the Tsumhpawng Ga area. Relying upon supplies by air, the enemy troops on the Taro Plain, in conjunction with the troops which had broken through the east side of the Wantuk Range, advanced toward the Division's left flank in the Yawngbang Ga area, and the situation became extremely critical.

Withdrawal to Maingkwan Area

Early in February, the Division ordered the 56th Infantry Regiment to counterattack, taking advantage of the enemy's advance to the bottleneck in the vicinity of Yawngbang Ga. Although this counterattack progressed well and achieved success, the Division's general strategic disposition became more unfavorable. The Division commander then decided that it was time to withdraw towards Maingkwan. This was done in mid-February.

The Division's original plan of the tactical disposition in the vicinity of Maingkwan was to attempt to establish the same type of aggressive defense as had been earlier contemplated at Taihpa Ga. However, it failed to materialize and an engagement between both forces was initiated about 20 February. A force, consisting of the Chinese 22d and 38th Divisions, attacked the Maingkwan position from the front and attempted to advance to Walawbum (at the rear of the Division) by making an enveloping movement on the right flank with an American force (Galahad). Late in February, enemy tanks appeared in front of the Japanese position but were repulsed by prepared protective fires. The Division received reports saying that on 1 March U.S. forces had suddenly appeared in the direction of Walawbum and the Division found itself completely enveloped by the enemy.

Retreat to Jambu Hkintang Mountains

On 2 March, the Division commander decided that he should contain the Chinese force with the 55th Regiment while the main strength of the division defeated the American force in the Walawbum area. This move was initiated on the following day, when the Nambyu River crossing point, strategic point for the division's withdrawal, had been taken by the enemy. At dawn on 4 March the 56th Regiment retook the crossing point and, in the evening, commenced an attack against the enemy near Walawbum. Enemy resistance was stubborn, troop strength was steadily reinforced, and the operations of the 18th Division did not develop satisfactorily. The Division commander, realizing that a continuation of the status quo would impede the accomplishment of the subsequent mission and in view of the fact that the Division was surrounded by the enemy, decided on 7 March to suspend the attack and withdraw to the line of the Jambu Hkintang Mountain Range. The withdrawal of the division from the Maingkwan-Walawbum area was accomplished by using two secret jungle trails, one of about 15 miles in length leading from Lalawng Ga to Jambu Hkintang and a shorter one from the Nambyu River crossing point to a point 2 miles south of Walawbum, which the 18th Engineer Regiment (commanded by Col. Miyama) had previously cleared. Although the Division had caused great damage to the enemy, as a result of continuous and incessant operations during the past four months, the losses which it had sustained were also heavy. Strength of infantry companies had decreased to 50 or 60, but the Division's defense mission was not reduced. Moreover, the proposed Imphal Operation, on which the hopes and fate of all the troops in Burma hinged, had not yet commenced. Regardless of difficulties and losses, it was the obligation of the Division to hold on the Kamaing-Mogaung line until the completion of the Imphal Operations.

Defense in Shaduzup Area

After conducting delaying actions in the vicinity of the Jambu Hkintang Mountain Range, the Division took positions on a line north of the confluence of several rivers in the vicinity of Shuduzup. (Map No. 8b). The engagement at this position commenced around 20 March with defense installations still incomplete. Although the enemy conducted daily tank attacks, mainly from the direction of the highway, the Division repulsed them with heavy losses. Meanwhile, the enemy attempted an enveloping movement from the upper stream of the Tanai River, and, late in March, troops of both sides in the right flank area became mixed up and an element of the enemy force penetrated deep into the rear area of Inkangahtawng on 23 March. Command liaison became increasingly difficult, and by the end of March the Division was compelled to withdraw its battle line approximately 10 kilometers to the south on a line extending east and west of Tingring.

An element of the Gallahad Force was driven from Inkangahtawng and surrounded at Nhpum Ga by a composite unit of the 114th Infantry Regiment from 28 March to 7 April, when the advance of the main body of the Gallahad Force broke the encirclement.

In mid-April, the 18th Division withdrew from the Tingring area to the Malakawng-Wala sector.

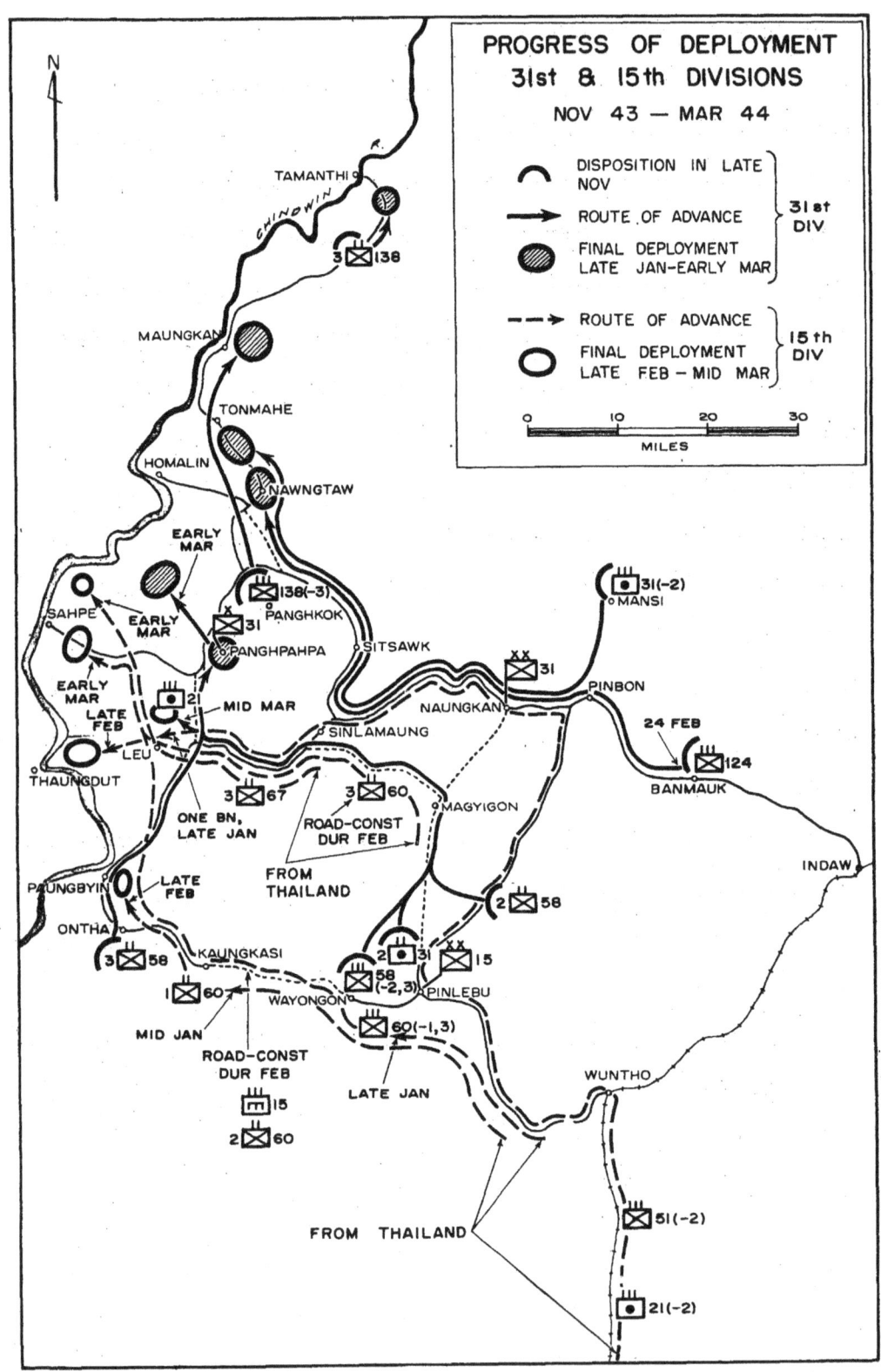

Conclusion of Hukawng Operation

Although the Division was still under the command of the 15th Army, after the commencement of the Imphal Operation, the 18th Division commander conducted operations in northern Burma almost at will. On 29 April when the 33d Army was organized, the 18th Division was placed in the order of battle of the new Army.

On 17 May, the Myitkyina airfield was occupied by elements of the Galahad force and on 28 May a Chinese detachment penetrated into the Japanese rear area to set up a roadblock at Seton.

The 18th Division having fought against a numerically superior force in the Malakawng-Wala front for about forty days, was finally forced to withdraw to Kamaing between 28 May and early June. Kamaing was the last important point to be held by the division, but the increasingly deteriorating situation did not permit a stand to be made there. The Hukawng Operation was concluded early in July by the withdrawal of the 18th Division from Kamaing.

Preparations for the Imphal Operation

15th Division: (Map No. 9)

The 15th Division, added to the 15th Army's order of battle on 17 June 1943, began to transfer from Shanghai in July and proceeded to Saigon in ten echelons. Placed originally under the direct control of the Southern Army, the Division was ordered to Bangkok in late August, arriving there about two months later. Further orders from the Southern Army directed the Division to advance elements to the Chiengmai area in the northwest part of Thailand to reconstruct the Chiengmai-Toungoo Road into a truck road. The Division formed a road reconstruction unit composed of one infantry battalion, two engineer regiments (including one attached engineer regiment) and two transport companies. Due to heavy rains and the difficulties of the steep terrain the road improvement was not completed.

In mid-October the Southern Army belatedly ordered the 15th Division to proceed to Burma without delay. The Division immediately concentrated its units in the Lampang area of Thailand and in early November ordered the advance unit (60th Infantry Regiment) to start the movement via the Chiengmai-Kengtung-Takaw Road. Although the Division had approximately ten motor transport companies, it did not make speedy progress and it was mid-January before the first of the advance units arrived in the area east of the Chindwin River. Two routes of advance over the Zibyu Range required reconstruction and improvement. The conversion of the Pinlebu-Kaungkasi-Paungbyin and Pinlebu-Magyigon-Sinlamaung Roads into cart roads was not completed before the Division was ordered to move to the Chindwin River, line of departure for the Imphal Operation. The accumulation of materiel had not progressed as expected and the advance units were forced to perform their defense duties for the first week or two while subsisting on a diet of gruel. Barely enough ammunition, provisions and forage for the offensive had been accumulated by early

March. The poor condition of the approach routes so seriously slowed the advance that the total force of the Division was unable to arrive at the river in time for the commencement of the river crossing operations.

The delay in the arrival of the 15th Division at the Chindwin was to prove one of the principal causes for the failure of the Imphal Operation.

31st Division: (Map No. 9)

In the 31st Division sector, efforts were concentrated on converting the Indaw-Pinbon-Homalin Road, the Sinlamaung-Paungbyin Road, and the Pinlebu-Pinbon Road into dry season motor roads. Toward the end of February the roads between Pinbon and Homalin, Homalin and Maungkan, as well as between Sinlamaung and Paungbyin were considered passable for motor traffic.

The Indaw and Wuntho areas had not been receiving supplies regularly until late November. Due to the move of the 18th Division to the Hukawng sector as well as the concentrated use of rail transportation for 31st Division troop movements, the railways were closed to the transport of supplies. Furthermore, since many bridges had been destroyed by bombing, regular supply by road was made much more difficult. In spite of these handicaps, the accumulation of a minimum amount of operational materiel was completed by March 1944. Approximately three weeks' rations, including emergency rations and those carried by the troops, were stored on the east bank of the Chindwin River. It was decided to carry ammunition for no more than three weeks of operations. Mountain guns, antitank guns and mortars were to be carried, but 105-mm howitzers were to be left behind. Equipment included a total of 17 mountain guns (two per company except the 9th Company). Because of very limited transportation facilities one half of the infantry guns and other heavy weapons organic to the infantry regiment were to be left behind.

Since the 31st Division would be required to cross the Chindwin River as well as the steep mountains and valleys of the Patkai Range in its advance to Kohima, special equipment to enable the Division to achieve its mission was needed. The combination of pack horses and motor vehicles, used in the past, was changed to a combination of pack horses and oxen. Although the Division was able to gather a total of approximately 3,000 horses and 5,000 oxen, only a three day supply of forage could be carried and it would then be necessary for the Division to depend on local sources.

In early December, the Division began to make final deployment for the coming offensive. By the end of February, troop disposition was virtually complete. In order to relieve the 31st Division of some of its areal responsibility, in late December, the 15th Army directed the 15th Division to take over the defense of the Chindwin River south of Homalin. In late January, the 31st Division units at Leu and Kaungkasi were each relieved by a battalion of the 15th Division.

33d Division:

In the 33d Division sector the road repair on the west bank of the Chindwin River had been nearly completed by the end of February. The Kalewa-Paluzawa-Mawlaik-Yazagyo Road had been completed for the use of heavy vehicles except between Mawlaik and Yazagyo, a distance of 25 miles. The Kalewa-Kyigon-Kalemyo Road and the Kyigon-Indaing gyi-Yazagyo Road had been entirely completed for the use of heavy vehicles. The Kalemyo-Fort White Road had been completed for heavy vehicular traffic except between Third Stockade and Fort White, a distance of 10 miles.

All munitions for operational purposes had been accumulated and stored between Mutaik and Shwegyin. Since most of the division's motor vehicles including those of the 33d Supply Regiment were used for transport between Yeu and Mutaik, the subordinate units were responsible for their own supply in the sector west of Kalewa. The transport of munitions across the Chindwin River did not progress as well as had been expected and even with the addition of supplies from the Kale Valley, barely enough provisions and forage were gathered prior to the commencement of operations.

Enemy Situation in Early 1944

At the beginning of 1944 there were positive indications of a forthcoming enemy counterattack along the entire Burma front. On the Mayu Peninsula, the British-Indian Army closed in on the 55th Division front at Buthidaung and Maungdaw. Furthermore, two to three divisions assembled around the Chittagong sector. On the Manipur front, there were three enemy divisions and other smaller forces in the vicinity of Imphal. Second line groups of approximately two to three divisions were advancing toward Shillong. The British-Indian 17th and 20th Divisions were advancing towards Tiddim and Tamu respectively, and the 23d Division was standing firm along the line from Imphal to the vicinity of Ukhrul, with an element advancing to the Fort White, Yuwa, Sittaung, and Homalin front. The construction of roads, transportation of river crossing materials and reconnaissance in force by the enemy on the eastern bank of the Chindwin River became increasingly active. Local enemy attacks on the Fort White, Yazagyo, and Mawlaik front became especially persistent. Furthermore, frequent intelligence was received to the effect that a powerful armored group was located in the vicinity of Imphal.

According to air reconnaissance, construction of large new airfields was progressing in the vicinity of Imphal, Palel and Tamu, and scores of enemy aircraft were seen at the Imphal and Palel air bases.

In eastern Assam the British 2d Division and another British-Indian division were in the Dimapur and Shillong areas. In addition, it was estimated that the enemy group in the Chittagong area would be moved whenever necessary to the Dimapur-Shillong area. There were strong indications that the main attack in this sector would be directed toward the Mawlaik area.

On the Hukawng front the strategic position of the 18th Division had become extremely critical. The Chungking Army in the Yunnan area was pushing preparations for a counterattack with extraordinary zeal. Intelligence reports indicated that they were bringing several additional divisions to Tali from the Chungking and Canton sectors and that units were being equipped with trench mortars and other new equipment. In addition, the strength of divisions was being increased to about 10,000 men. In order to transport river crossing materials and to stock-pile provisions and forage, work was being done to maintain strategic roads leading from Paoshan to crossing points on the Salween River. It was estimated that preparations were progressing to the point where the enemy would be able to launch a counterattack in a few months.

Air superiority over almost all of Burma had fallen to the enemy by early 1944, and rail and vehicular traffic was already becoming impossible during daylight hours. Enemy air attacks on air bases, strategic communication points and important military installations in central and northern Burma became extremely persistent.

The number of enemy secret agents equipped with radios in central and northern Burma was increasing and their operations were intensified.

Estimate of the Situation

In view of the enemy counteroffensive preparations in the various areas, it was estimated that the enemy was planning to recapture all of Burma by launching a diversionary attack on the Mayu Peninsula, while directing his main counterattack toward central and northern Burma. British, United States and Chinese forces would then converge on the Mandalay sector. As the main attack progressed, a powerful counterattack would be launched from the sea towards southwestern Burma. Burma Area Army Headquarters and the 5th Air Division were greatly concerned with the possible enemy sea attack and there was some difference of opinion with the 15th Army estimate of the situation.

The situation in Burma at the close of 1943 was marked by tension as both sides prepared for the battle to come. The 15th Army had not yet gained approval for the invasion of Imphal and the 15th Division was still at the Thailand-Burma boundary.

Final Plans for the Imphal Operations

From 22 to 26 December 1943, the 15th Army held a conference to again consider the possibility of carrying out the U-Go Operation and to develop detailed missions for each division by means of a war game.

Lt. Gen. Naka, Chief of Staff of the Burma Area Army, and Lt. Gen. Ayabe, Vice-Chief of Staff of the Southern Army, attended. Based upon the results of this conference, the Southern Army intended to make its final decision on the Imphal Operation.

General Ayabe eventually made the decision that, from both strategical and tactical points of view, it was essential to the defense of Burma to hold the general line of Kohima and the high ground west of Imphal and that, even if there were risks inherent in the plan, it should be carried out.

Approval by Imperial General Headquarters

The Commander-in-Chief, Southern Army, accepted the views of General Ayabe and early in January 1944 sent him to Tokyo to obtain the sanction of Imperial General Headquarters (IGHQ) for the proposed offensive. There, Ayabe was asked five questions:

    1. Could the Southern Army deal successfully with an Allied seaborne attack from the Bay of Bengal in the midst of the U-Go Operation?

    2. In view of the increased length of the front which would result from the occupation of Imphal, was there sufficient strength to guarantee the continued defense of Burma?

    3. Could the small Japanese air force keep pace with the ground forces and support them throughout the operation?

    4. Was the supply position satisfactory?

    5. Could the 15th Army's plan be relied on?

Apparently satisfied by General Ayabe's replies to their questions, on 7 January 1944, IGHQ assented to the proposed operation and issued Army Directive No. 1776:

> In order to defend Burma the Commander-in-Chief, Southern Army, may occupy and secure the vital areas of north-eastern India, in the vicinity of Imphal, by defeating the enemy in that area at an opportune time.

Despite the expressed approval, IGHQ apparently still had some qualms as to the wisdom of the operation, for on the following day in a message to the Southern Army the need for careful control of the operation to bring it to a favorable conclusion at the earliest possible moment was stressed and a warning was sounded against a possible enemy offensive toward the southwest coast.

In accordance with the IGHQ directive, on 15 January, the Southern Army issued an order to the Burma Area Army to proceed with the Imphal (U-Go) Operation. In turn, the Area Army issued an order on 19 January briefly announcing the general objective of the operation:

> To destroy the enemy at Imphal and establish strong defense positions covering Kohima and Imphal before the coming of the rainy season.

The 56th Division was placed under the direct command of the Area Army in order that the 15th Army might concentrate on the operations on the western front. The 18th Division was to remain under the 15th Army until late April 1944 when it would be assigned to the new 33d Army which was to be activated in northern Burma.

15th Army Attack Orders

On 25 January, the 15th Army commander summoned the chiefs of staff of the divisions under his command to a conference and issued orders for the strategic deployment of the Army forces. He also generally outlined his plan for the crossing of the Chindwin River. Crossings would be made by means of motor and row boats, bamboo rafts and all other available craft which could be made ready by D-1 Day. One element of the 31st Division would cross the river near Tamanthi and the main force near Homalin. The 15th Division main force would cross in the vicinity of Paungbyin. All combat troops would be moved across the river between nightfall of D Day and daybreak of D + 1 Day. Vehicles and rear units would commence crossing by pontoon rafts during and after the second night of the movement. Upon the successful completion of the crossing of the combat troops, all attacking columns would immediately initiate offensive advances.

Because of the limited strength of the 5th Air Division, the Army could not expect direct air support for the ground operations. However, the Army could rely on the Air Division conducting decisive air combat missions and indirectly facilitating ground operations. The Army requested that the Air Division maintain control of the skies above the Chindwin River at the time of the crossing operation. The Air Division was also expected to perform reconnaissance of enemy movements in the Imphal Plain as well as to assist in the transport of supplies as might be required in the course of the operation.

On 11 February the 15th Army issued an attack order based on the following revised operations plan:

    1. The 15th Division will, by early March complete preparations on the banks of the Chindwin River. Starting the offensive on D Day from the area between Homalin and Sittaung, the Division will move through the enemy troops into the mountain district northwest of the Imphal Plain and rush to the sector west of Imphal. At the time a part of the Division will be detailed to cut the Kohima-Imphal Road and the Bishenpur-Silchar Road. (Map No. 10).

    2. The 31st Division will complete preparations on the Chindwin River by early March, Starting the offensive on D Day from the area between Tamanthi and Homalin, the Division will strike at Kohima moving though Fort Keary and Layshi. With a powerful element the Division will strike at Kohima along the Ukhrul-Kohima Road. The Division, after occupying Kohima, will cut off enemy reinforcements expected from Dimapur, and cover the flank and rear of the main force of the Army until the capture of Imphal has been completed. (Map No. 10).

    3. The 33d Division will launch an offensive along the Tiddim-Moirang and the Tamu-Palel Roads; followed by a surprise crossing of the Chindwin River by the 15th and 31st Divisions. Subsequently, the 33d Division will double back upon the enemy in the Imphal Plain and attack from the south simultaneously with an attack by the 15th Division from the north. Meanwhile the 31st Division will occupy Kohima and block off the enemy from that direction.

    4. The 33d Division will advance with its main force to the edge of the Chin Hills, west of Kalemyo, and the vicinity of Yazagyo in the Kabaw Valley by late February and will complete preparations for the start of an attack on this line. On D-7 Day the Division will commence an offensive drive to Imphal, repulsing the enemy in the area along the road connecting Fort White,

MAP NO. 10

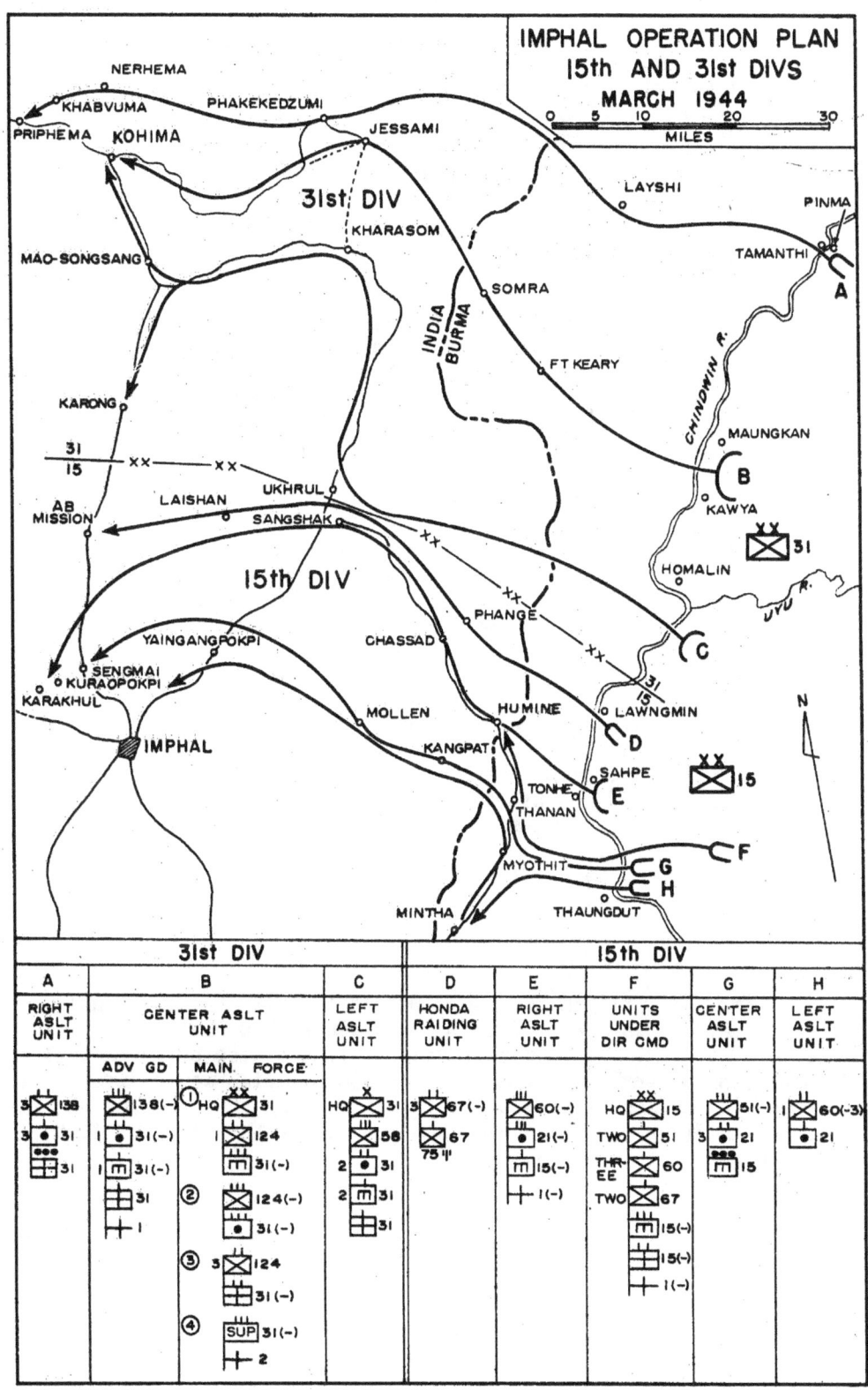

Tonzang, Churachandpur, Bishenpur and Imphal. In addition, a strong detachment with heavy field artillery, tanks and antitank guns as its nucleus will rush through the Kabaw Valley and, breaking up the enemy counterattack which may be anticipated in the plains area, will advance toward Tamu and then move against Imphal along the Tamu-Palel-Imphal Road in coordination with the Division's main force. (Map No. 11)[3]

5. The capture of Imphal will be completed by mid-April. Thereafter, the mountain ranges east of Dimapur and Silchar and the Chin Hills will be secured and the necessary defense preparations made before the advent of the rainy season.

6. In order to keep the projected offensive secret, the 15th and 31st Divisions will not take any action, including reconnaissance, on the west bank of the Chindwin, and will limit the number of units advanced to the banks of the river prior to the actual commencement of the offensive.

7. Each division will provide for its own supply along the respective advance routes until the occupation of Imphal. Thereafter, the Army will execute supply via the Kalewa-Tamu-Imphal Road and use the previous routes as auxiliary supply lines.

8. D Day will be 15 March 1944.

---

3. The 33d Division had been ordered to initiate an offensive prior to that of the Army's main force because that Division would be required to make the longest advance. It was also believed that by initiating an earlier offensive, the 33d Division would divert the enemy in the Imphal area thereby facilitating the crossing of the Chindwin River and the subsequent strikes by the 15th and 31st Divisions.

MAP NO. 11

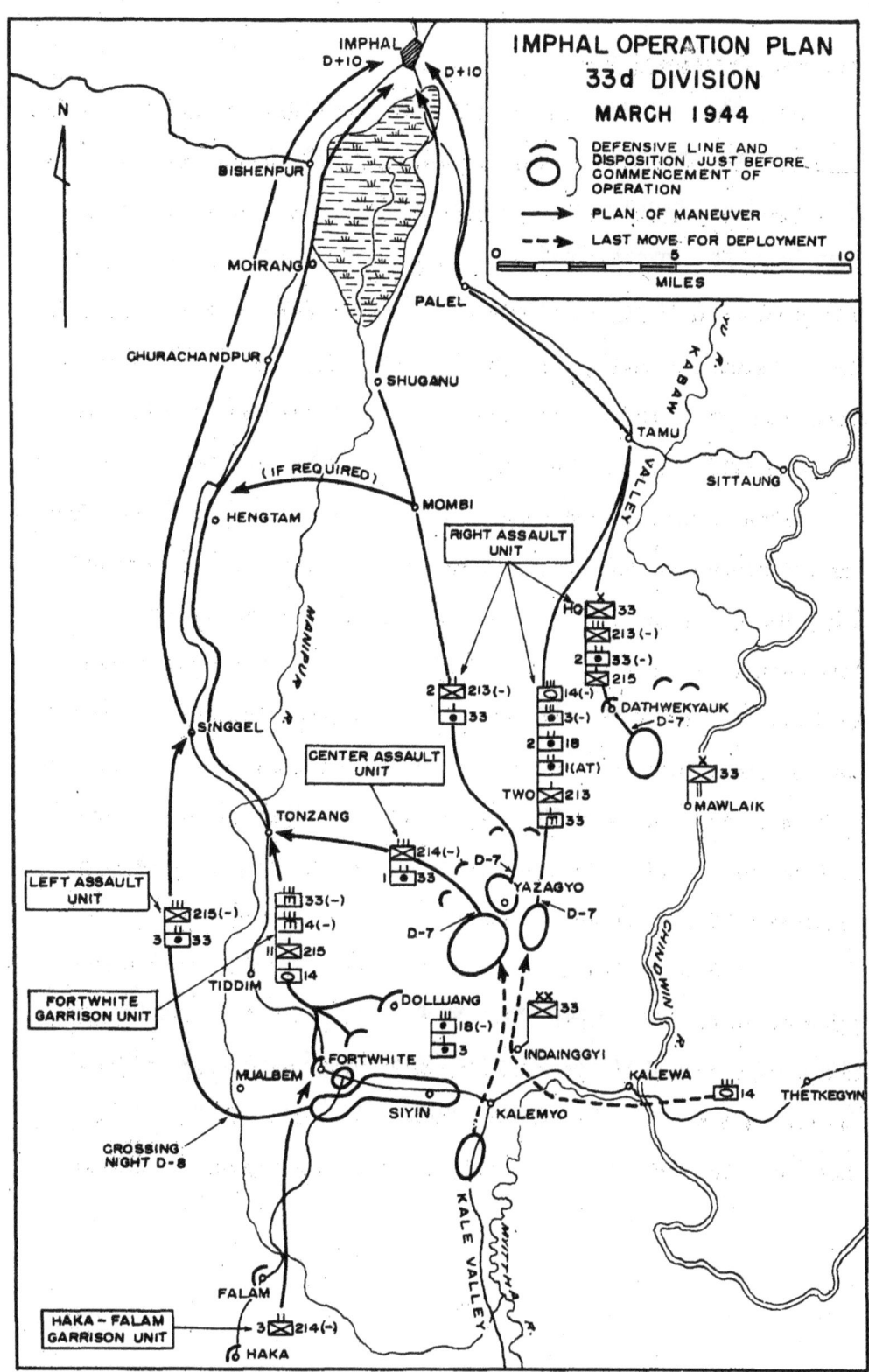

Tactical Considerations

The rainy season, which lasts from the middle of May to the end of September, reaches its peak during July and August when all rivers overflow their banks and vehicular traffic is seriously disrupted. Therefore, the invasion had to be completed by the middle of April and a new defense line established and reinforced by the middle of May. Thereafter, during the peak of the rainy season, large scale enemy counterattacks in the mountain zone of the India-Burma border would be difficult, although air raids could be expected.

Allowing for all reasonable delays, it had been concluded that the offensive must be launched some time between mid-February and early March, since an offensive launched earlier might invite a large-scale counterattack prior to the advent of the rainy season. However, because of the distances involved, the 15th Division would not be able to complete deployment and preparations by the beginning of March. The Army decided, therefore, to concentrate on the preparations of the 15th Division and to launch the offensive as early in March as the progress of the Division would allow.

The success of the Imphal Operation was dependent upon a surprise assault. If the plan were to be divulged before its execution, the crossing of the Chindwin River would meet with stubborn resistance supported by superior enemy air power. It was evident that the bold tactics of the Army, aimed at the capture of Kohima and Imphal within three weeks by making a long march across the steep Manipur Mountains, could be upset by well prepared enemy resistance and reinforcements from the eastern Assam area. There was also the possibility that efforts of the 55th Division to contain the enemy in the south might not be effective.

Concealment of Intentions

As emphasized in the operations plan, the 15th Army took several precautionary measures to maintain the secrecy of the operation. The defense line on the east bank of the Chindwin River was obviously bolstered by employing natives to work on defense positions and much progaganda was spread by the secret operating teams in the area. The advance of troops to the Chindwin River was restricted, river crossing operations were concealed and reconnaissance of the west bank sector prohibited. The enemy was held on the 33d Division front by feigning the presence of the main body of the 15th Army and it was planned to advance the 1st Infantry Regiment of the INA to Haka and Falam to feign an attack on Aijal. These moves were calculated to deceive the enemy into thinking that the Army was going to attack Chittagong in concert with the 55th Division. Troop movements were performed during the hours of darkness and maximum concealment was achieved by dispersion and by utilizing the cover offered by the dense jungle.

As the divisions of the 15th Army made last minute preparations for the Imphal Operation, the enemy became extremely active on the 33d Division front. The British-Indian 20th Division advanced from Tamu toward Sittaung and Mawlaik and the 17th Division became active in both the Fort White and Dollaung areas. An enemy force which had moved from the sector north of Yazagyo along the Kabaw Valley Road, launched a combined infantry, artillery and air attack against the advance position of the 213th Infantry Regiment, north of Mawlaik, forcing the advance force to withdraw.

Operations Plan of the 15th Division (Map No. 10)

The 15th Division was to advance to the hill area northwest of Imphal, whence the attack on Imphal would be made in coordination with the 33d Division, advancing from the south.

Task Force Organization

The Division also organized task forces for the accomplishment of its mission:

Hq. 15th Division

    Cmdr: Lt. Gen. Masabumi Yamanouchi

Honda Raiding Unit

    Cmdr: Maj. Honda, CO, 3d Bn, 67th Inf Regt
    3d Bn (less two cos), 67th Inf Regt
    Regtl Gun Co, 67th Inf Regt
    Elm, 15th Engr Regt

Right Assault Unit

    Cmdr: Col. Matsumura, CO, 60th Inf Regt
    60th Inf Regt (less 1st Bn and two cos)
    21st Fld Arty Regt (less 2d and 3d Bns).....
                    6 type 31 Mt Guns
    Two plats, 15th Engr Regt
    Half of 1st Fld Hosp

Center Assault Unit

    Cmdr: Col. Omoto, CO, 51st Inf Regt
    51st Inf Regt (less 2d Bn, 1st and 2d Cos)
    3d Bn, 21st Fld Arty Regt ..... 3 Mt Guns
                  (Type-31)
    Elm, 15th Engr Regt

Left Assault Unit

    Comdr: Maj. Yoshioka, CO, 1st Bn, 60th Inf Regt
    1st Bn (less 3d Co), 60th Inf Regt
    One btry, 21st Fld Arty Regt
              1 Mt Gun (Type-31)
    Elm, 15th Engr Regt

Unit under direct command of the Division

    15th Div HQ
    Div Sig Unit
    Two cos, 51st Inf Regt
    Three cos, 60th Inf Regt
    Two cos, 67th Inf Regt
    Suisei Co (a composite unit)
    15th Engr Regt (less one co and four plats)
    Div Armorer Unit
    Div Med Unit
    Half of 1st Fld Hosp

Attack Order

Specific tasks were assigned to each of the assault units:

    1. The Honda Raiding Unit will cross the Chindwin River near Lawngmin on the night of D Day and will advance via Phange, Ukhrul and Laishan to cut the Kohima-Imphal Road at Mission.

2. The Right Assault Unit will cross the Chindwin River near Sahpe on the night of D Day and will advance to the Karakhul-Kuraopokpi area via Humine, Chassad and Sangshak.

3. The Center Assault Unit will cross the Chindwin River near Thaungdut on the night of D Day and advance to Sengmai via Thanan, Kangpat and Mollen.

4. The Left Assault Unit will cross the Chindwin River near Thaungdut on the night of D Day and will advance first to Mintha to cover the left flank of the Division. Later the unit will advance to the north of Imphal via Thanan, Mollen and Yaingangpokpi.

5. The 15th Engineer Regiment (less elements) will be engaged initially in implementing the river crossing operations of the Division. Upon completion of that phase of the operation, the Regiment will engage in road construction across the Minthami Mountains under the command of the Army Construction Unit.

6. The units under the direct command of the Division will cross the Chindwin River near Thaungdut and will advance in the rear of the Center Assault Unit in the initial stages of the march and will later follow the Right Assault Unit.

Operations Plan of the 31st Division (Map No. 10)

The 31st Division was to rush directly to Kohima to block the road connecting Dimapur, Kohima, Mission, and Imphal. After the occupation of Kohima, the Division was to have one element pursue the enemy toward Dimapur while the main force re-grouped to hold Kohima and vicinity.

Task Force Organization

The Division re-organized into three assault units to accomplish its mission:

Hq. 31st Division

Cmdr: Lt. Gen. Kotoku Sato

Right Assault Unit

Cmdr: Maj. Shibazaki, CO, 3d Bn, 138th Inf Regt
3d Bn, 138th Inf Regt
3d Btry, 31st Mt Arty Regt
One plat, 31st Engr Regt
Elm, Div Med Unit

Center Assault Unit

Advance Guard

Cmdr: Col. Torigai, CO, 138th Inf Regt
138th Inf Regt (less 3d Bn)
1st Bn (less 3d Btry), 31st Mt Arty Regt
1st Co (less one plat), 31st Engr Regt
Elm, Div Med Unit
1st Fld Hosp

Main Force (in order of march)

1st Ech: 1st Co, 124th Inf Regt
Div Sig Unit
Div Hq
1st Bn (less 1st Co), 124th Inf Regt
31st Engr Regt (less 1st and 2d Cos)

2d Ech: 124th Inf Regt (less 1st and 3d Bns)
31st Mt Arty Regt (less 1st and 2d Bns)

3d Ech: 3d Bn, 124th Inf Regt
Div Med Unit (less 2/3)

4th Ech: 31st Sup Regt (less one co)
2d Fld Hosp

Left Assault Unit

    Cmdr: Maj. Gen. Miyazaki, CG, 31st Inf Gp
    Hq, 31st Inf Gp
    58th Inf Regt
    2d Bn, 31st Mt Arty Regt
    2d Co, 31st Engr Regt
    Elm, Div Med Unit

Attack Order

Missions for each of the assault units were assigned as follows:

   1. The Right Assault Unit, completing preparations by D-7 Day at Pinma, will cross the Chindwin River near Tamanthi during the night of D Day and will advance to Priphema by way of Layshi, Phakekedzumi, Nerhema and Khabvuma to cut the Dimapur-Kohima Road.

   2. The Center Assault Unit, completing preparations in the sector between Maungkan and Kawya by D-7 Day, will cross the Chindwin River in the following order: Advance Guard on the night of D Day; then the 1st, 2d, 3d and 4th Echelons will cross on the next succeeding four nights. The unit will then advance to Kohima through Fort Keary, Somra and Jessami.

   3. The Left Assault Unit, completing preparations in the sector south of the confluence of the Chindwin and Uyu Rivers by D-7 Day, will cross the Chindwin River in the sector below Homalin on the night of D Day and will advance to Kohima by way of Ukhrul, Kharasom and Mao-Songsang. An element will be dispatched south to cut the Imphal-Kohima road at Karong.

Operations Plan of the 33d Division (Map No. 11)

Task Force Organization

The 33d Division was to approach Imphal from the south and launch the main attack. For the offensive, the Division was organized into task forces which were termed assault units. The task force organization was established as shown below:

Hq. 33d Division

    Cmdr: Lt. Gen. Genzo Yanagida

Right Assault Unit

    Cmdr: Maj. Gen. Yamamoto, CG, 33d Inf Gp
    Hq. 33d Inf Gp
    213th Inf Regt (less 1st Bn)
    5th Co, 215th Inf Regt
    14th Tk Regt (less 5th Co)
    1st AT-Gun Bn (less 1st and 2d Cos)
    2d Bn, 33d Mt Arty Regt
    3d Hv Fld Arty Regt /less 2d Bn, 2d Btry
      (less one plat) and ½ Regt Ammo Tn/
    2d Bn, 18th Hv Fld Arty Regt
    1st Co, 33d Engr Regt

Center Assault Unit

    Cmdr: Col. Sakuma, CO, 214th Inf Regt
    214th Inf Regt /less 3d Bn (less 9th and
      10th Cos)/
    1st Bn, 33d Mt Arty Regt
    Element, 33d Engr Regt

Left Assault Unit

    Cmdr: Col. Sasahara, CO, 215th Inf Regt
    215th Inf Regt (less 5th and 11th Cos)
    3d Bn, 33d Mt Arty Regt
    Element, 33d Engr Regt

Fort White Garrison Unit (Front Assault Unit)

    Cmdr: Col. Yagi, CO, 33d Engr Regt
    33d Engr Regt (less two cos and one plat)
    4th Indep Engr Regt
    11th Co, 215th Inf Regt
    5th Co, 14th Tk Regt

Haka-Falam Garrison Unit

   Cmdr: Maj. Tanaka, CO, 3d Bn, 214th Inf Regt
   9th and 10th Cos, 214th Inf Regt

Artillery Unit

   Cmdr: Col. Mayama, CO, 18th Hv Fld Arty Regt
   18th Hv Fld Arty Regt (less 2d Bn)
   One plat, 3d Hv Fld Arty Regt

Attack Order

Coincident with the formation of the assault units the Division issued its attack order:

   1. The Right Assault Unit will start its advance on D-7 Day from the sector north of Mawlaik with its main force and from the vicinity of Yazagyo with one element. After having annihilated the enemy in the vicinity of Witok, Moreh and Tamu, the Unit will strike at Imphal via Palel. An element, with one infantry battalion as its nucleus, will proceed from Yazagyo to Imphal via Mombi and will be prepared to turn from Mombi to Hengtam to cooperate with the Center Assault Unit. In order to conceal offensive plans, the advance of the 14th Tank Regiment to the Chindwin River will be performed after 1 March by strictly controlled night marches.

   2. The Center Assault Unit will transfer from its assembly area south of Kalemyo to the district south of Yazagyo as secretly as possible. The Unit will start its advance on D-7 Day and will strike first at Tonzang. After annihilating the enemy there, the Unit will move toward Imphal parallel to, and east of the Tonzang-Imphal Road.

   3. The Left Assault Unit will cross the Manipur River in the vicinity of Mualbem on the night of D-8 Day, strike at Singgel and cut off the enemy's route of retreat from Tonzang. From there the Unit will strike at Imphal, moving

parallel to, and west of the Singgel-Imphal Road. In interrupting the retreat of the enemy north of Tonzang, an element will be dispatched to the bridge across the Manipur River, north of Tonzang, to hold it as long as possible.

4. The Fort White Garrison Unit will hold the line connecting Dolluang, Pimpi and Fort White and will support the Left Assault Unit in its crossing of the Manipur River. Thereafter, the Unit will assume the offensive and strike at Tonzang in concert with the Center Assault Unit. The Unit will also repair the Kalewa-Imphal Road between Fort White and Tonzang so that it may be utilized by the Artillery Unit.

5. The Haka-Falam Garrison Unit will hold the Haka-Falam line and defend the vicinity of Fort White with an element after the Fort White Garrison Unit shifts to the offensive.

6. The Artillery Unit will occupy a position south of Fort White and make preparations to check any counterattack of the enemy. The Unit will also cooperate directly with the Fort White Garrison Unit in the latter's offensive, but no artillery support will be given unless absolutely necessary to check a major counterattack by the enemy. The Unit will advance along the Kalewa-Imphal Road to cooperate with the Center and Left Assault Units.

7. The Division Signal Unit will maintain radio contact between each assault unit and Division headquarters and establish and maintain a wire network along the Kalewa-Imphal Road, starting at Fort White.

8. Each unit will carry provisions for 14 days and will endeavor to collect and utilize local commodities. Efforts will be exerted to economize on ammunition. For infantry weapons, the basic load will be allotted. For artillery, an amount up to three units of ammunition will be available (a one-month campaign supply). Captured weapons and ammunition will be collected and utilized whenever possible.

CHAPTER 3

THE IMPHAL OPERATION

The Wingate Airborne Invasion

On 9 March 1944, with the Imphal offensive under way, 15th Army Headquarters was informed that on the 5th an enemy airborne unit had landed in the area north and southeast of Katha.

Reconnaissance by the 5th Air Division indicated that the airborne unit was a fairly powerful force and it was estimated that the its objective was to establish an air base and be gradually reinforced by air. The 5th Air Division launched a series of attacks on 10 March and Col. Suzuki, Chief of Staff of the Air Division considered the airborne invasion threat so serious that he recommended reconsideration of the Imphal Operation. Some staff officers of the 15th Army also recommended postponement of the operation until the airborne unit could be wiped out. General Mutaguchi, however, believed that the invasion was a diversionary attack presaging an approaching counterattack on the western front and felt that the execution of the Imphal Operation was more necessary than ever. In addition, the 15th Army did not believe that the airborne unit was as powerful as had been indicated by the 5th Air Division and thought that the force could easily be contained and repulsed.

The 15th Army took steps to destroy the invading force with various small units which were immediately available. These units were grouped under the command of Lt. Col. Nagahashi as the Nagahashi Unit, a provisional composite battalion consisting of some 18th Division troops which were in the vicinity and the 3d Battalion, 114th Infantry Regiment, which was en route from Kyaukme to Myitkyina.

The Burma Area Army agreed that the Imphal Operation should be carried out as scheduled but took a more serious view of the strength and potentialities of the Wingate Airborne Force. As more information became available, the 15th Army also became convinced that the Wingate Force might be a greater threat than had originally been thought. Just prior to D Day of the Imphal Operation, in addition to the Nagahashi Unit, the following units were ordered to the general area of the Wingate invasion force:

Sent Toward Mawlu

2d Bn, 51st Inf Regt, 15th Div	-From Hsipaw via Mandalay
2d Bn, 146th Inf Regt, 56th Div	-From Wanting via Myitkyina
2d Bn, 21st Fld Arty Regt, 15th Div	-From Hsipaw via Mandalay
1st Co, 213th Inf Regt, 33d Div	-From Pakokku
12th Co, 146th Inf Regt, 56th Div	-From Lashio via Mandalay

Sent to Napin

Hq 67th Inf Regt	-From Wuntho
2d Bn, 67th Inf Regt	-From Wuntho

About the middle of March the Area Army sent the main body of the 24th Mixed Brigade from Moulmein and several 2d Division units from the Bassein area to reinforce the 15th Army in its operations against the Wingate invasion force. The 24th Mixed Brigade, commanded by Maj. Gen. Hayashi, had a strength of 1,874 and was composed of the following:

    Two companies - 139th Inf Bn
    Two companies - 141st Inf Bn
    One company - 138th Inf Bn
    One battery - Brig Arty Unit
    Two platoons - Brig Engr Unit
    Brig Sig Unit (One-half)

The 2d Division units were the 4th Infantry Regiment (less 3d Bn) and the 2d Battalion, 29th Infantry Regiment. Approximately one month later the 2d Battalion, 2d Field Artillery Regiment of the 2d Division was also sent from Bassein.

Two small scale attacks launched against the Wingate perimeter in mid-March from a point about one mile north of Mawlu were unsuccessful. Meanwhile the various units were assembling in the Indaw area. On 25 March Maj. Gen. Hayashi, CG, 24th Mixed Brigade, was designated to take command of all ground operations against the airborne invasion force.

Start of the Imphal Offensive

The 15th Army began its main offensive toward Imphal while discussions were still being held regarding the possible affects of the enemy airborne raiding force. The 33d Division began movement of its units on 7 March (D-8) and on 15 March (D Day) the 15th and 31st Divisions succeeded in crossing the Chindwin River without meeting any major opposition. Each group crossed the frontier and began advancing in accordance with prearranged plans.

The 33d Division-March and April (Map No. 12)

Elements of the Left Assault Unit moved into the sector north of Mualbem and in cooperation with the Fort White Garrison Unit, covered the Manipur River crossing of the main force of the Unit. The crossing was successfully accomplished on the night of 7 March and the Left Assault Unit advanced along a mountain path, west of the Manipur, to Singgel. On 14 March, the Unit cut the Tonzang-Imphal Road at Point 3299 and at Singgel. One company of the 215th Infantry Regiment, which was dispatched to hold the Manipur River bridge north of Tonzang, was annihilated.

Since February, the Fort White Garrison Unit had been subjected to several heavy attacks but had succeeded in repulsing them. Beginning about March 10th, the enemy became so active that it appeared that an over-all attack would be launched in the Fort White area.[1]

---

1. It was later determined that the enemy's repeated attacks were made in an effort to conceal an attempted withdrawal.

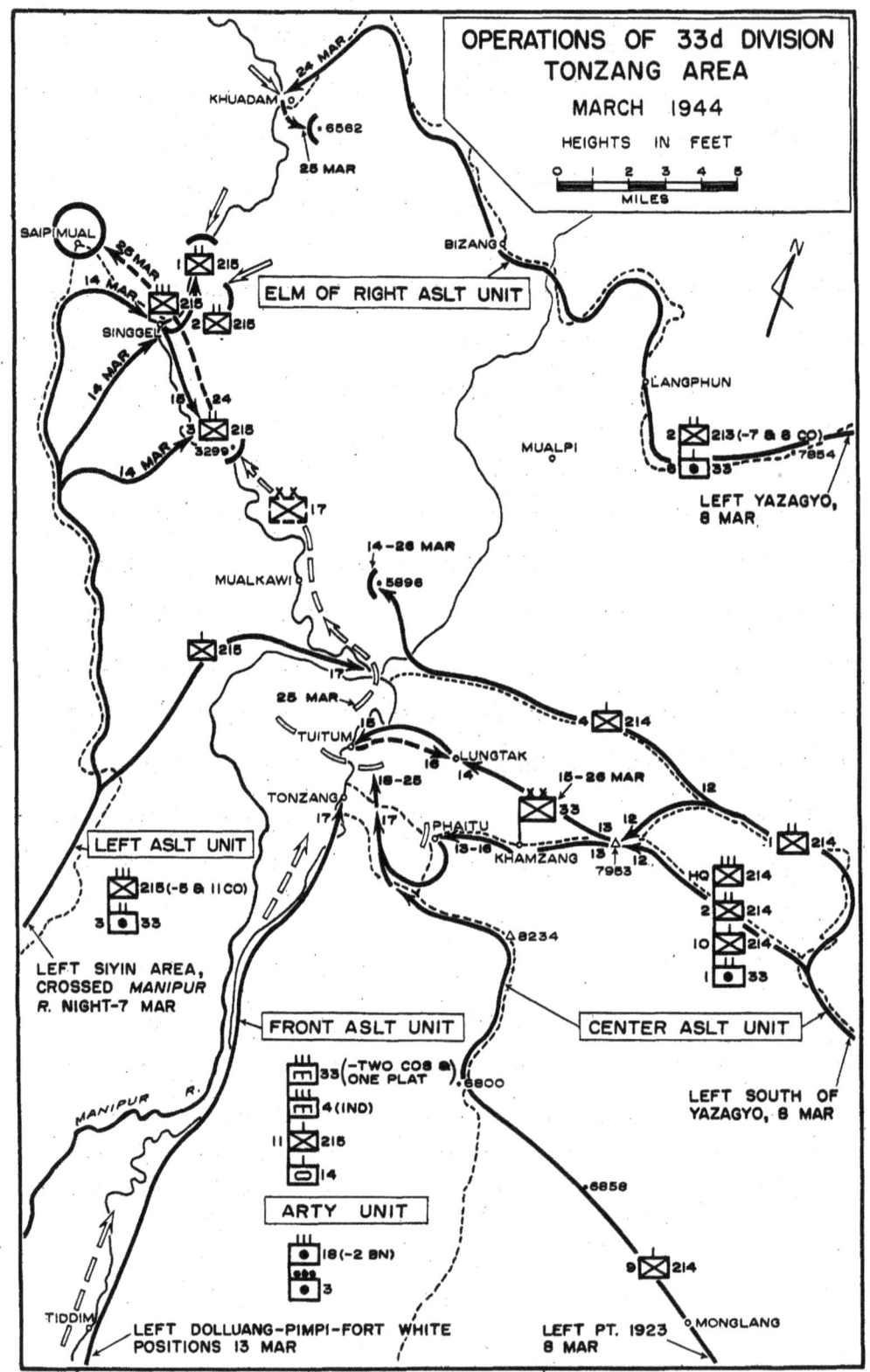

On 13 March the Garrison Unit shifted from the defense to the attack and subsequent pursuit of the enemy, which at first offered stubborn resistance. However, with the Garrison Unit's advance from Dolluang to the vicinity of Kennedy Peak, north of Fort White, the enemy began a more rapid withdrawal. The Fort White Garrison Unit, under the commander of the 33d Engineer Regiment, then became the Front Assault Unit and advanced to the vicinity of Tonzang, via Tiddim, on 17 March. In the meantime, efforts were being made to remove the antitank land mines which the enemy had planted on the Fort White-Tonzang Road and to reconstruct the road to accommodate heavy vehicles.

Operations in the Tonzang Area

The Center Assault Unit which moved out from Yazagyo on 8 March, reached the vicinity of Hill 7953 on 12 March after having constructed a pack horse road through the steep Chin Hills. On Hill 7953 the enemy had established a strong defense position of the type known to the Japanese as a "Honeycomb Defense", composed of many small, interlocking and mutually supporting cells. With the support of the attached mountain artillery the Center Assault Unit attacked and penetrated the position on 13 March. One company (4th Co, 1st Bn, 214th Inf Regt) advanced to Hill 5896 on the 14th and the 1st Battalion (less the 4th Co), 214th Infantry moved toward Tonzang via Tuitum. On the 15th the Battalion encountered an enemy position at Tuitum.

Owing to disadvantageous terrain and poor conduct of the action, the Battalion was obliged to withdraw east toward Lungtak. The 1st Battalion's mission was one of the most important in this phase of the operation and its failure to penetrate the Tonzang defenses gave the enemy an opportunity to withdraw across the Manipur River. The 4th Company, which had advanced to Hill 5896, was bypassed by the enemy and was ineffective in preventing or delaying the enemy withdrawal.

Meanwhile, on 14 March, the main force of the Center Assault Unit launched an attack on Phaitu but, failing to dislodge the defenders, bypassed the position and advanced to the area east of Tonzang on 17 March.

As a result of the rapid advances of the Center, Front and Left Assault Units, by 15 March the British-Indian 17th Division was completely encircled and contained in the sector between Tonzang and Singgel. In a desperate effort to check the advance of the assault units, the enemy division offered stubborn resistance in positions north of Tonzang. In addition, during the period 17 through 24 March, the enemy made strong counterattacks against the Left Assault Unit in an attempt to break the encirclement and withdraw toward Imphal via Singgel. During the time of encirclement, the enemy was supplied chiefly by air.

The Center and Front Assault Units initiated night assaults on the withdrawing enemy's rear guard position at Tonzang on 18 March but the efforts failed to disrupt the defenses. Subsequently, the

Center Unit conducted nightly raids for the next week, continuing until the first line battalion had lost approximately one-third of its strength. Finally, on the 25th of March, the enemy rear guard began a withdrawal and the Center Assault Unit pursued toward Mualkawi.

By the 18th of March the Fort White Garrison Unit, operating as the Front Assault Unit, had advanced to the vicinity of Tonzang and from the 18th of March participated in the attacks on the enemy positions in cooperation with the Center Unit. Upon the withdrawal of the enemy on 25 March the Front Assault Unit also advanced toward Mualkawi.

Although the Artillery Unit had advanced to a sector just south of Tonzang by 19 March, it was prevented from lending support to the assault units because of enemy artillery and air activity and because of the necessity to conserve ammunition for future operations.

Encirclement of the Enemy

By seizing the Imphal Road, north and south of Singgel, the Left Assault Unit had cut off the enemy's route of retreat. The British-Indian 17th Division made a number of desperate counterattacks in an effort to effect a withdrawal and reinforcements were rushed from the Imphal area in an effort to break through the encirclement. Because of the heavy pressure being brought to bear on the Left Assault Unit, Col. Sasahara, the Unit commander, determined to annihilate the encircled enemy. He sent a battle report to Division Headquarters outlining his intentions and as evidence of his firm determination, ended the message in a dramatic manner:

> ".....The Left Assault Unit will hold roadblocks in Singgel to the last. The code books will be burned, if necessary."

Unfortunately, due to faulty communications facilities, Division Headquarters received this latter part of the message well before receiving the first part of the message. Misunderstanding the situation, Division Headquarters erroneously believed the Left Assault Unit to be in desperate straits. Therefore, on 24 March, the Left Assault Unit was directed to withdraw from the Singgel area and assemble to the west. Compliance with this order caused the 33d Division to lose the opportunity of completely destroying the 17th Division.

Although the envelopment of the enemy 17th Division had been accomplished by the separate advances and coordinated actions of the assault units, the 33d Division failed to maintain the encirclement. The basic cause of the failure to capitalize on its advantage was due to the Division commander being out of contact with his units and being unable to exercise unified control over them. In addition, the 214th Infantry Regiment, the key force of the Center Assault Unit, missed advantageous opportunities by launching a series of ineffectual attacks. As a result of these tactic and because of the withdrawal of the Left Assault Unit, the enemy was able to withdraw to the Imphal Plain to reinforce the enemy in that area.

Suggested Suspension of Offensive

The 33d Division commander, advancing at the rear of the Center Assault Unit, assumed tactical command of the Division in the vicinity of Khamzang on 15 March and advanced to Mualkawi with the Center Assault Unit on the night of March 26th.

At this point, with the other divisions of the 15th Army steadily advancing against little opposition the 33d Division commander, suddenly suggested the suspension of the Imphal Operation. He strongly recommended that the present defense positions be held and strengthened and justified his reluctance to advance against Imphal in a message to 15th Army Headquarters which was worded approximately as follows:

> 1. The combat situation of the Center Assault Unit is not developing satisfactorily and discouraging reports are coming in from the Left Assault Unit.[1] In the future the offensive will encounter such extreme difficulties that the occupation of Imphal within the scheduled three weeks is an impossibility. In addition, the advent of the rainy season and difficulties of supply will eventually result in tragedy.
>
> 2. Our organization and equipment are inferior to that of the enemy and since recent fighting and the rigors of the advance have reduced the fighting power of our troops, the capture of Imphal is virtually impossible.

---

1. The results of later investigation revealed that the losses sustained by the Left Assault Unit were only about 15 per cent of its total strength. It is probable that the Division commander was strongly influenced in his pessimistic attitude because of misunderstanding the report received from the 215th Infantry Regimental Commander, Col. Sasahara. Auth.

3. The landing of parachute units in the Katha area endangers all of Burma, which has now been practically stripped of troops.

   4. The strategic value of Imphal has been exaggerated.

The Army commander was at a loss to understand the reluctance of the 33d Division commander to continue an offensive which was being so well executed. The suggestion of General Yanagida was considered inappropriate and he was directed to execute the Army's orders. At the end of March, therefore, the Division commander ordered further advance and continued attack.

The failure of the 33d Division commander to display the proper aggressive spirit caused the Army Staff to become apprehensive. It was recognized that the Division, which constituted the main force for the attack on Imphal, in hesitating for ten days in the vicinity of Tonzang and then being overly cautious in its advance had made the capture of Imphal, within the scheduled time, most improbable. In addition, the fact that the British-Indian 17th Division had been permitted to escape reduced the chances for the success of the operation.

Drive Toward Tengnoupal

The Right Assault Unit, later known as the Yamamoto Detachment, initiated an advance on 8 March from the sector north of Mawlaik with its main force and from the sector north of Yazagyo with an element (Map No. 11). On 13 March the Mitsui Unit: composed of the 3d Heavy

Field Artillery Regiment (less the 2d Battalion and half the Regimental Ammunition Train); the 2d Battalion, 18th Heavy Field Artillery Regiment; the 14th Tank Regiment; two companies of the 213th Infantry Regiment and one engineer company; attacked Witok (Map No. 13). The 2d Battalion (less two companies), 213th Infantry Regiment (with the 6th Battery, 33d Mountain Artillery Regiment attached), was directed to change its course at Mombi and proceed in the direction of Kuadam for the purpose of cooperating with the Left and Center Assault Units (Map No. 12). Late in March the Battalion was placed under the command of the Left Assault Unit.

Maj. Gen. Yamamoto, estimating that the enemy was about to withdraw, dispatched the Ito Unit: composed of the 3d Battalion, 213th Infantry Regiment; the 2d Battalion (less the 6th Battery), 33d Mountain Artillery Regiment and one engineer platoon to cut off the enemy's route of retreat in the vicinity of Sibong or Chamol. The Ito Unit advanced to Chamol on 25 March over a mountain trail but failed to block the routes at Chamol Fork because of strong enemy counterattacks. The 11th Company (3d Battalion, 213th Infantry Regiment), displayed great fortitude in holding Nippon Hill from 26 March until it was wiped out on 11 April.

The Left Assault Unit of the 15th Division (1st Battalion, 60th Infantry Regiment and one battery, 21st Field Artillery Regiment) was transferred to the Right Assault Unit of the 33d Division. On 20 March it moved south from Mintha and made an unsuccessful attack on

MAP NO. 13

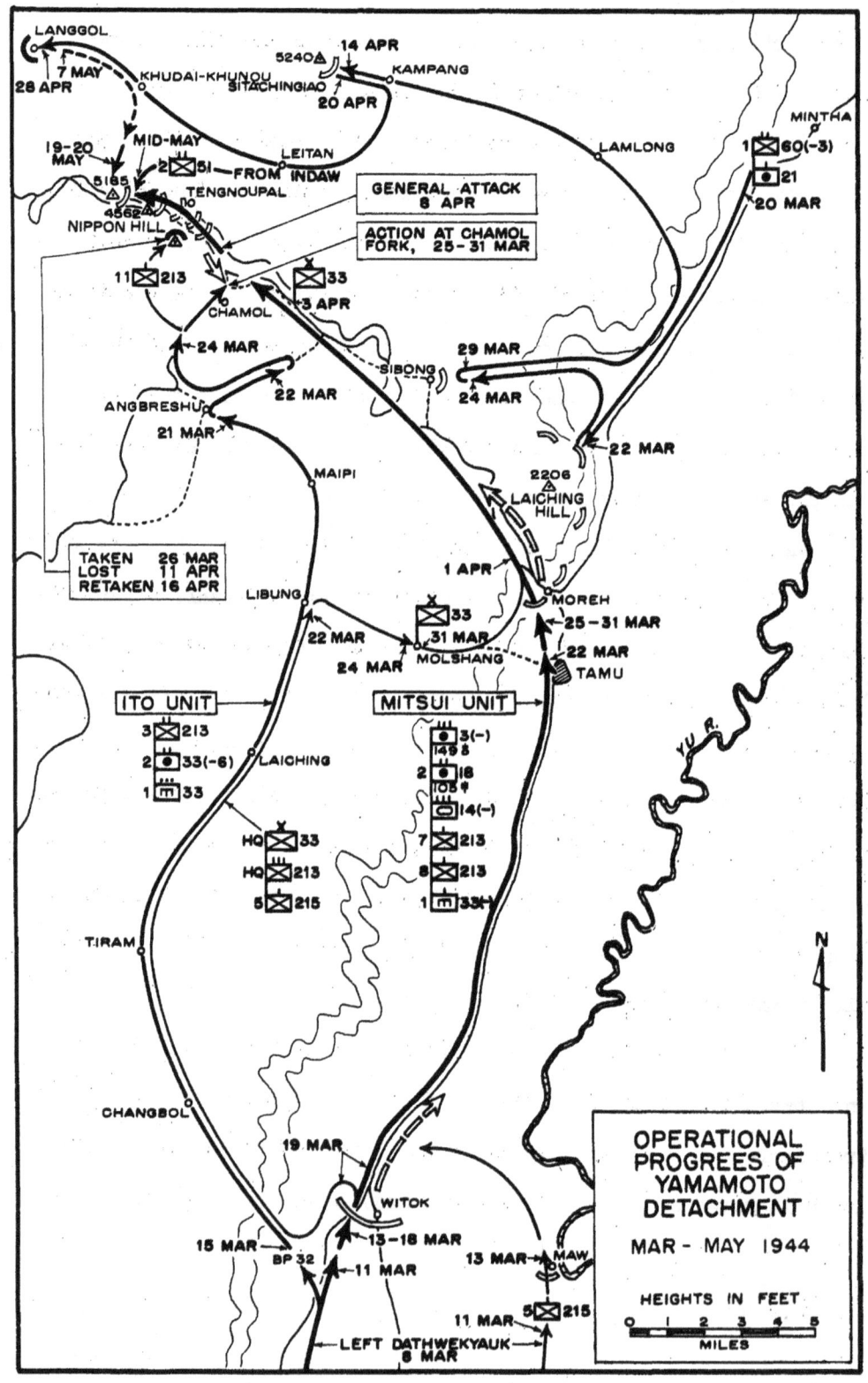

Laiching Hill on 22 March.

Meanwhile, after seizing Witok on 18 March, the Mitsui Unit advanced to Tamu on 22 March. The enemy troops near Moreh had entrenched themselves in a well prepared circular position. Starting on 25 March, the Mitsui Unit initiated a series of attacks with tanks and heavy artillery but had made little progress when the enemy withdrew on 31 March. The Right Assault Unit was placed directly under the Army command in late March and was redesignated the Yamamoto Detachment.

Taking advantage of the steep terrain along the Tengnoupal-Shenam Pass and their prepared defensive positions, enemy troops attempted to halt the advance of the Yamamoto Detachment. The Detachment launched an attack on 8 April and by dogged perseverance moved into the enemy position almost foot by foot. When on 7 May, the 3d Battalion, 213th Infantry Regiment, finally captured Hill 4562 west of Tengnoupal, the combat potential of the 213th Infantry had been stretched almost to the limit.

Meanwhile, on 20 April, the 1st Battalion, 60th Infantry Regiment, which had failed in its attack on Laiching Hill in March and had also made an unsuccessful attack against Sitachingiao in mid-April was given the mission of penetrating into the sector north of Palel. On April 28th, the Battalion entered Langgol but was forced to withdraw on 7 May.

Early in May, the Yamamoto Detachment was reinforced by the 2d Battalion, 51st Infantry Regiment, which had been engaged in operations against Wingate. On the night of 19 May, the Battalion, in coordination with the 1st Battalion, 60th Infantry Regiment made an assault on Hill 5185 (Laimatol Hill) and although it was successful in seizing the hill, was forced to relinquish it the following day after suffering heavy casualties. From then on a stalemente developed with neither of the three battalions nor the enemy making any important moves.

Operations Toward Bishenpur (Map No. 14)

Anticipating an enemy counterattack from Moirang, the Division commander selected this as an intermediate assault objective instead driving direct to Bishenpur.

After replenishing ammunition and provisions expended at Tonzang, the Center Assault Unit left Mualkawi on 29 March and, entering the steep mountainous zone between the Imphal Road and the Manipur River, continued to advance. Meeting little enemy resistance, the Unit crossed the India-Burma border on 5 April and arrived south of Churachandpur on 10 April.

The Left Assault Unit had also expended much of its ammunition and provisions but was able to replace them mainly with captured material. After infantry and artillery ammunition had been resupplied, the Unit left Singgel on 27 March and, breaking through the enemy

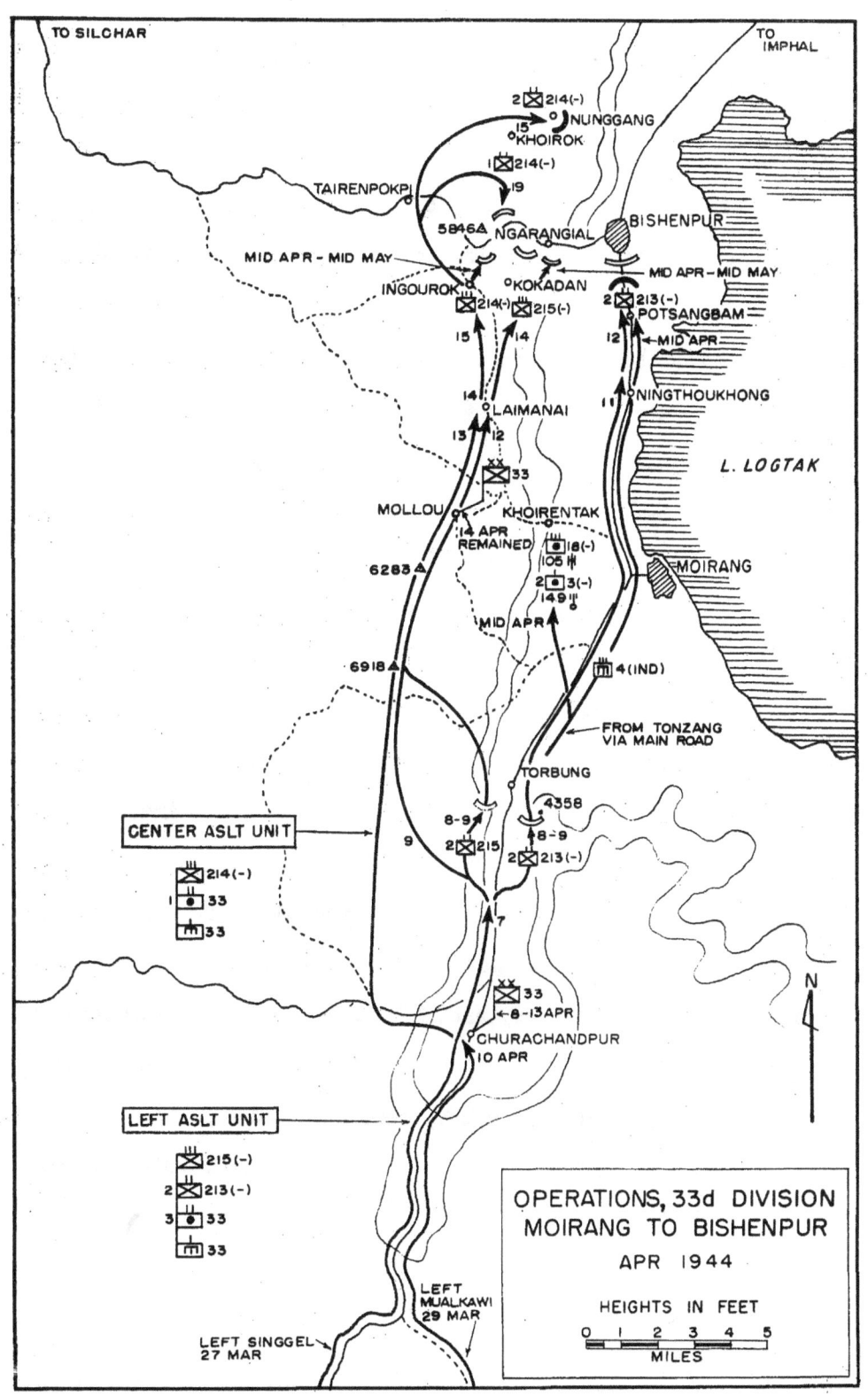

rear guard position near Chikha on 2 April, advanced across the India-Burma border on 3 April, reaching the sector north of Churachandpur on 7 April.

The Artillery Unit advanced to the vicinity of Churachandpur on 11 April, following the Left Assault Unit and repairing the roads destroyed by the enemy.

On 8 April the commander of the 33d Division was informed that the main force of the 15th Division had advanced to the sector northeast of Imphal and that the 31st Division had occupied Kohima on 6 April. Consequently, in order to advance quickly to the Imphal Plain, the commander decided to by pass the expected enemy resistance in the vicinity of Moirang and protect his rear by maintaining strong points in the mountain zone to the west.

Elements of the Left Assault Unit prepared to attack an enemy force at the entrance to the defile south of Torbung on 9 April but, finding that the enemy had already withdrawn, the Unit immediately pursued. The 2d Battalion, 213th Infantry Regiment attacked the enemy in Ningthoukhong and Potsangbam and advanced to the northern end of Potsangbam Village on 12 April. Thereafter the situation became a stalemate, held up by enemy artillery fire from Bishenpur defenses.

The 215th Infantry Regiment advanced to Kokadan on the morning of 14 April and, for about a month, made repeated attacks on enemy positions south of Ngarangial but were unable to penetrate the positions.

On the morning of 15 April the Center Assault Unit advanced to Ingourok through the mountains. An enemy force in positions on Mori Hill, south of Point 5846, checked three attacks by the 214th Infantry Regiment between 15 and 24 April. A reinforced battalion of the Regiment bypassed Point 5846 in an effort to penetrate the enemy position from the rear. This maneuver was also unsuccessful.

On 15 April the Artillery Unit began advancing its units to the area of Khoirentak to support the 214th and 215th Regiments. The 4th Independent Engineer Regiment was brought up to reinforce the 2d Battalion, 213th Infantry at Potsangbam about 20 April.

On 22 April, General Mutaguchi, CG, 15th Army, personally visited the headquarters of the 33d Division and spent several days in an effort to spur the Division to greater efforts. Since the unsatisfactory conduct of the 33d Division in the Tonzang area, General Mutaguchi had lost faith in its commander, Lt. Gen. Yanagida. During his visit, Mutaguchi virtually ignored Yanagida and devoted his time to working with Col. Tanaka, the Chief of Staff. From that time on, Col. Tanaka, in effect, commanded the Division by direction of General Mutaguchi.

The British-Indian 17th Division had occupied the outer perimeter of Bishenpur, but the village itself was occupied by a brigade of the 20th Division. This disposition had been effective since just before the beginning of the attack by the Center and Left Assault Units in the middle of April. The defenders had constantly improved their positions and by the middle of May had achieved a very strong defensive zone honeycombed with trenches and surrounded by several wire entanglements.

The 15th Division - March and April (Map No. 15)

Immediately after crossing the Chindwin River, the assault units of the 15th Division began advancing along their assigned routes and, although some enemy resistance was encountered, the Division advanced steadily to the Kabaw Valley.

On March 20th, the Left Assault Unit, which had advanced to Mintha, was ordered to turn south toward Moreh to cooperate with the Right Assault Unit of the 33d Division and this Unit did not thereafter participate in the operations of the 15th Division.

Cutting the Northern Approaches to Imphal

The 15th Division made a succession of rapid advances but its combat strength was extremely low. The infantry companies averaged only about 100 men each, while the Division possessed only nine Type 41 and nine Type 31 mountain guns.

The Honda Raiding Unit (built around the 3d Battalion of the 67th Infantry Regiment), advancing through gaps in the enemy lines and overcoming steep terrain, attained its objective of intercepting the Imphal-Kohima Road by seizing Mission and vicinity on 28 March.

MAP NO. 15

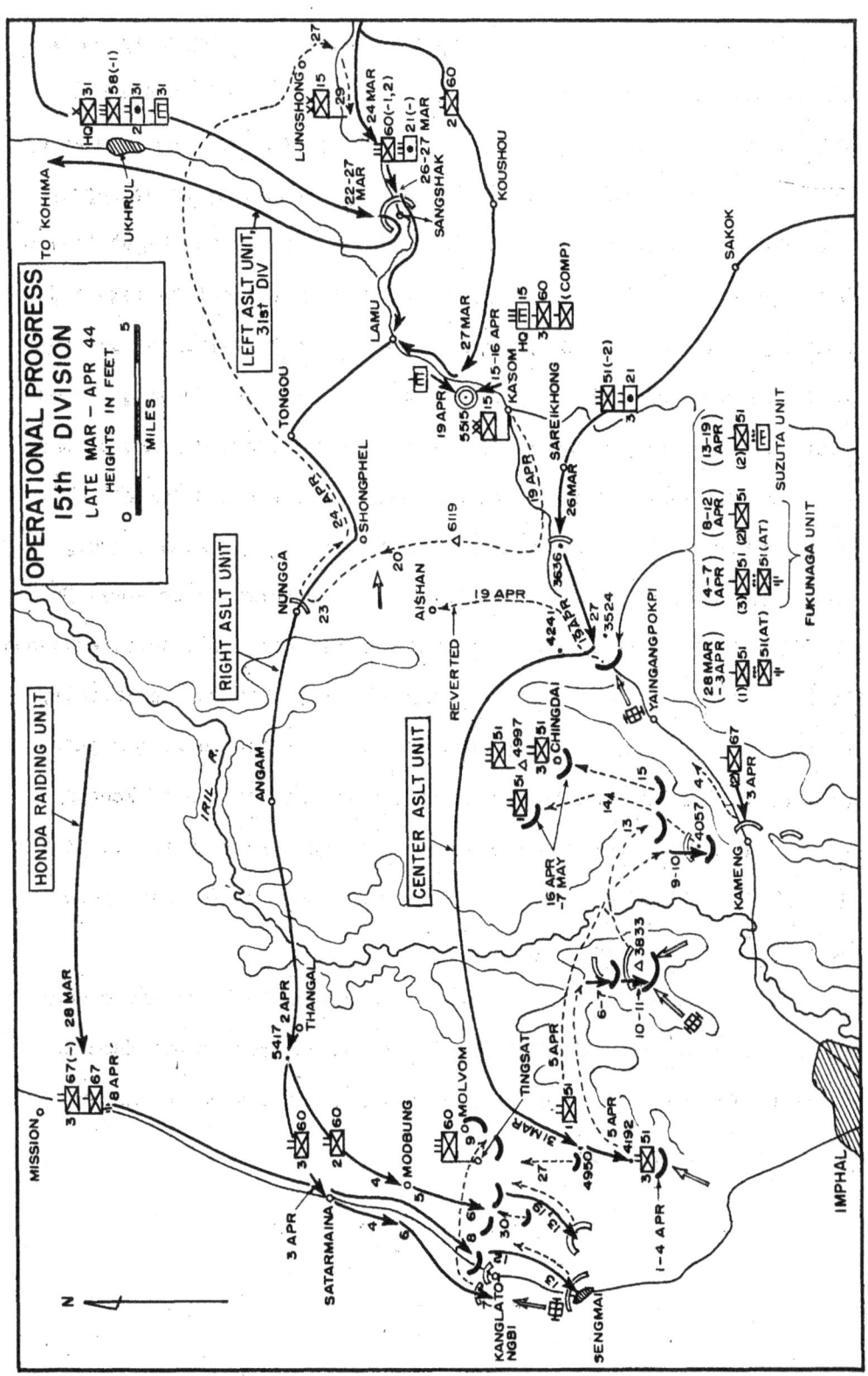

The Right Assault Unit advanced to the east of Sangshak on 24 March, via Humine and Chassad. Since 22 March, the Left Assault Unit of the 31st Division had been attacking Sangshak where an enemy force of approximately brigade strength was defending in well-prepared defense positions. Col. Matsumura, commanding the Right Assault Unit, ordered the 3d Battalion, 60th Infantry Regiment to make a dawn attack on March 26th. He also directed the 2d Battalion of the 60th to launch a coordinated attack from the direction of Koushou. Preparations required postponement of the attack for one day and on the night of the 26th the enemy force withdrew. The Right Assault Unit then continued its advance through Lamu, Tongou, Shongphel, Nungga and Angam cutting the Imphal-Kohima Road at Satarmaina on April 3d.

The Center Assault Unit, encountering little resistance, advanced to Hill 4950, four miles east of Sengmai, on 31 March. An infantry company and an antitank gun platoon had been stationed at the pass near Hill 3524, east of Yaingangpokpi, with the mission of keeping the Imphal-Ukhrul Road under control. The Center Assault Unit took Hill 4192 on 1 April and completed preparations for further operations toward Imphal by 3 April.

Division Headquarters advanced to Kasom on 28 March and ordered two companies of the 67th Infantry to attack and occupy Kameng. The attack was made on the night of 3 April but failed to achieve its objective.

In spite of occasional minor reverses, it now appeared that both the Right and Center Assault Units would reach their initial objectives, and be prepared for the coordinated drive on Imphal, in accordance with prearranged plans. However, the Division felt that its strength was spread too thin and was well aware that the detachments holding along the Imphal-Ukhrul Road were badly in need of bolstering. To remedy the situation, the Division decided to bring both assault units into closer contact and, by April 4th, move into positions north of Imphal. The Right Assault Unit would move to Sengmai and the Center Assault Unit along a line between Points 3833 and 4057.

Attacks on Sengmai

In the Sengmai sector the 2d Battalion, 60th Infantry Regiment took the hills east of Kanglatongbi on 6 April, but the 3d Battalion sustained losses of 68 men KIA in an engagement with enemy tanks in the area west of Kanglatongbi on the 7th. On 8 April, the Right Assault Unit together with the Honda Raiding Unit took up positions between Molvom and Tingsat, north of Kanglatongbi and proceeded to prepare for further operations.

On the night of 12 April an unsuccessful attack was made on Sengmai by the Honda Unit and the 2d Battalion, 60th Infantry. In a second attack, made on the 18th, the 2d Battalion gained a foothold in the enemy positions on a hill east of Sengmai but were forced to relinquish their gains after suffering approximately 150 casualties.

The failure to breach the enemy defenses at Sengmai marked the turning point in the operation and from that time on the Right Assault Unit was on the defensive.

Redeployment East of the Iril River

The Center Assault Unit moved east from Hill 4950 on the night of 5 April. The 3d Battalion, 51st Infantry Regiment captured an enemy position north of Hill 3833 on 7 April and seized the entire hill on 11 April. There the Battalion held against repeated enemy counterattacks in which tanks played a major part. The 1st Battalion, 51st Infantry captured Hill 4057, north of Kameng, on 10 April and also held against several enemy counterattacks. The strong enemy pressure, however, took a heavy toll of the 51st and companies were reduced to 20 or 30 men each. Col. Omoto, CO, 51st Infantry Regiment, realizing that the Regiment could not continue to take such terrific losses and still remain effective, suggested to Division Headquarters that, since it would be impossible for the Regiment to hold both sides of the Iril River, every effort should be made to hold the sector east of the river. On April 12th the Division commander, agreeing with Col. Omoto, gave the 51st the mission of holding the mountainous area east of the Iril River and preparing for a further offensive. At dusk on the 12th, the 3d Battalion withdrew from Hill 3833 and took up positions in the hills north of Hill 4057. From this position the 3d Battalion provided cover to permit the 1st Battalion to withdraw from Hill 4057 on the night of the 13th. The Center Assault Unit then proceeded to strengthen its positions and remained on the defensive in the vicinity of Chingdai from 16 April to 7 May.

Enemy Counterattacks on the Division Rear

Along the Imphal-Ukhrul Road, enemy counterattacks had been constantly harassing the Fukunaga Unit, a provisional group composed of elements of the 51st Infantry Regiment, which had the mission of holding the pass near Hill 3524. The Fukunaga Unit held its positions by keeping continuous pressure on the enemy counterattacking groups. On 12 April, Capt. Fukunaga, commander of the Unit was replaced by Lt. Col. Suzuta, the Division Adjutant, and the Unit was redesignated the Suzuta Unit. Meanwhile another enemy group suddenly appeared in the rear of Division Headquarters and established positions at Hill 5515, north of Kasom, on 15 April. A composite unit of Headquarters troops with a strength of about 200 twice attacked the position without success. At the same time the Suzuta Unit was faced with a serious crisis when it was attacked by a strong enemy tank force on 18 April.

With his headquarters threatened by this new enemy maneuver, the Division Commander decided to move 15th Division headquarters and the Suzuta Unit to the rear of the Right and Center Assault Units. This move was complicated in that it entailed the evacuation of large numbers of casualties, among whom was General Yamanouchi. Upon arriving in the vicinity of Nungga intense enemy activity was encountered. It was found impossible to move west, to the desired destination and the headquarters was forced to move toward Lungshong via Ukhrul. The Suzuta Unit troops reverted to their parent organizations. The command post of the Division was finally established at a point about three miles southwest of Lungshong on 29 April.

The 31st Division - March and April

The front line troops of the 31st Division executed the crossing of the Chindwin River on the night of 15 March and, meeting only weak enemy resistance on the west bank, forced an advance in accordance with plans. The Right and Center Assault Units advanced against light resistance to Layshi and Jessami, and about 7 April the leading troops of both columns reached the sector east of Kohima. (Map No. 10)

In general, the advance of the Division was relatively smooth, but the transportation of supplies through the rugged mountain ranges was extremely difficult. Stocks of provisions dropped to low levels and there was a shortage of forage for the pack animals. Almost all the requisitioned oxen dropped dead during the passage of the mountains and the loss of horses was about 16 per cent for the artillery and about 60 per cent for other units. The men also suffered from exhaustion and malnutrition. Several hundred who were afflicted with beriberi were left behind at the Molhe Collecting Station.

Attack on Sangshak.

After crossing the Chindwin, the Left Assault Unit arrived at Ukhrul on 21 March where contact was made with a British unit. Reconnaissance indicated that the enemy unit was approximately one brigade, was equipped with heavy artillery and occupied positions at Sangshak. Although Sangshak was outside its operational boundaries the Unit believed it could quickly inflict an overwhelming defeat on the enemy and the decision was made to attack on 22 March. The task proved much more difficult than had been estimated and the Left Assault Unit did not occupy the British position until March 26th, when the defending troops withdrew. The fact that the Left Unit lost some 16 per cent of its strength and spent five days in the Sangshak engagement undoubtedly had an adverse affect upon the final operation at Kohima. Meanwhile, the 1st Battalion, 58th Infantry Regiment which had been dispatched from Ukhrul on 24 March as the leading echelon, defeated an enemy group at Tuphema, just south of Kohima, and cut the Imphal-Kohima Road on 30 March.

Occupation of Kohima

The main body of the Left Assault Unit advanced to Maosongsang on 3 April, where the following disposition was made: 1st Battalion, 58th Infantry, via Maram to Pulomi, 13 miles west of Maosongsang; the 3d Battalion, 58th Infantry via Chakhabama to Kohima and the balance of the Unit to Kohima along the Imphal-Kohima Road. (Map No. 16)

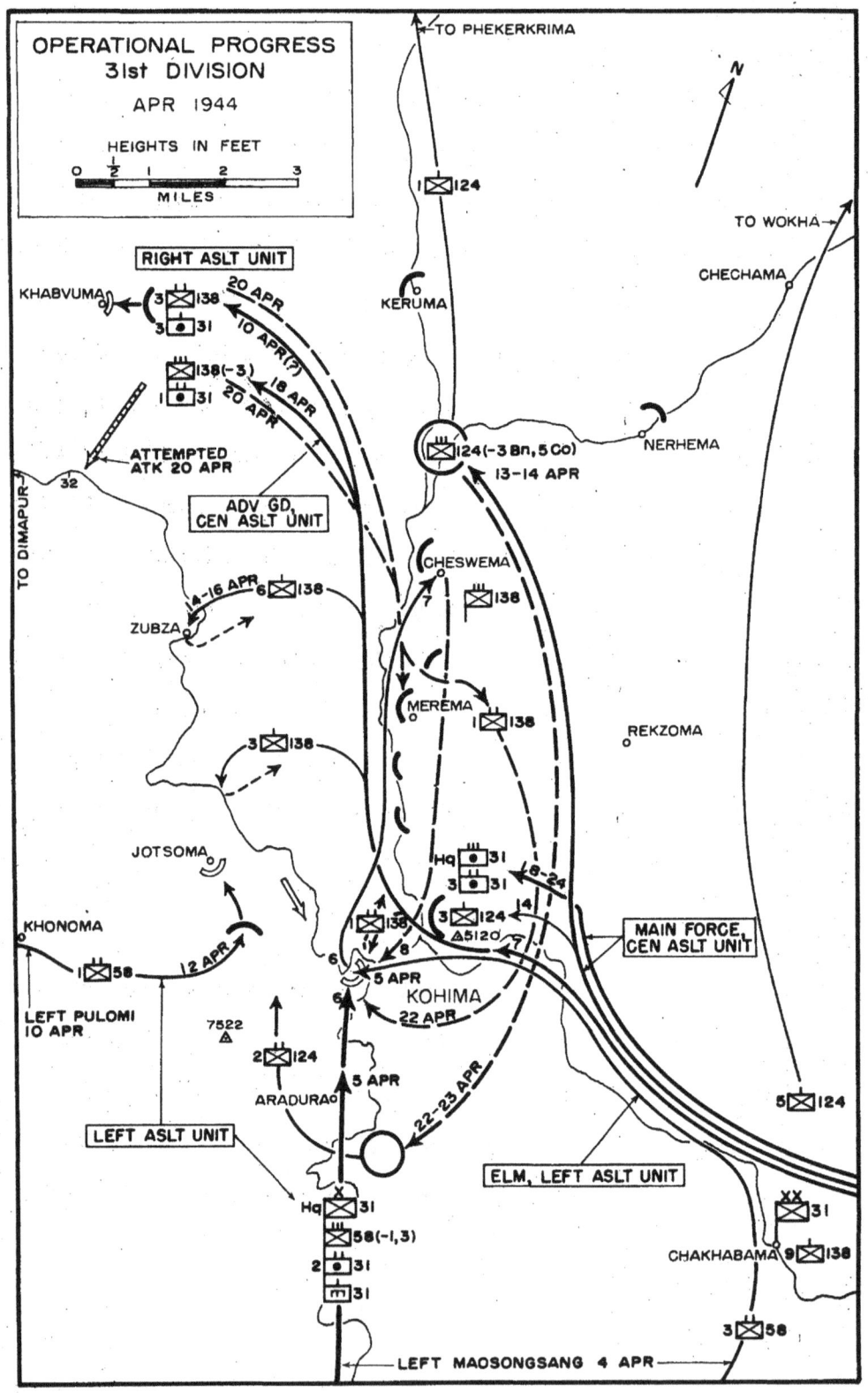

On the morning of April 5th, the 3d Battalion, 58th Infantry Regiment, seized the old town of Kohima in a surprise raid and occupied Garrison Hill before sunset. Maj. Gen. Miyazaki, commanding the Left Assault Unit, assumed that the enemy had withdrawn from Kohima and ordered the 3d Battalion to advance to Cheswema. This proved to be a serious error, for as soon as the 3d Battalion had left on the morning of 6 April, Garrison Hill was immediately occupied by the British. When the 2d Battalion, 58th Infantry made an attempt to retake the hill on the evening of the same day, they found the enemy strongly entrenched on the hill and a desperate battle immediately developed. The 3d Battalion was called back from Cheswema and the 1st Battalion of the 138th Infantry which had arrived at Kohima on April 7th, as the lead unit of the Center Assault Unit, was also thrown into the attack.

The Division commander, believing that the capture of the hill would shortly be effected, turned his attention to the more pressing business of preventing the enemy from reinforcing Kohima from the northwest. The 138th Infantry Regiment (less the 3d Battalion) was given the mission of cutting off the Kohima-Dimapur Road in the vicinity of Zubza. The Division was also concerned with possible enemy activity from the direction of Mokokchung and the 124th Infantry Regiment was moved from Chakhabama to the vicinity of Cheswema to prepare for operations to the north. The 3d Battalion of the 124th was directed to remain and defend the town of Kohima. The main body of the 31st Mountain Artillery Regiment, which had been about ten days behind its scheduled time in crossing the Chindwin River, arrived at Kohima around 20 April and established positions in support of the attack against Garrison Hill. In the meantime, the Left Assault Unit launched determined attacks against the hill fortifications. The British defenders, well entrenched and supported by air, resisted with equal determination.

Attempts to Cut the Kohima-Dimapur Road

On 12 April the 1st Battalion of the 58th Infantry approached Jotsoma from Pulomi but, in spite of repeated attacks, could not penetrate the enemy position. The 138th Infantry Regiment which had been given the mission of cutting the Kohima-Dimapur Road at Zubza also failed in its mission because unfavorable terrain prevented their achieving the objective with the strength available. The 6th Company (2d Bn, 138th Inf Regt) did succeed in penetrating the enemy position at Zubza and seriously disrupted the defense. However, the 2d Battalion was unable to capitalize on this achievement and the 6th Company, with only nine survivors, was forced to retire.

The 1st Battalion of the 138th Infantry which was attacking north of Jotsoma was caught in concentrated cross fires while making attack preparations and was forced to abandon its attack although the 3d Company achieved some success in breaking up enemy dispositions on the main road.

The Right Assault Unit (3d Bn, 138th Inf Regt) made an unsuccessful attack on Khabvuma and found itself facing a strong enemy detachment in the sector east of the village. About April 15th, the 1st and 2d Battalions of the 138th Infantry moved to the area southeast of Khabvuma and joined the Right Assault Unit and made an attempt to cut the Kohima-Dimapur Road near Mile 32 on 20 April.

In mid-April, traffic on the Kohima-Dimapur Road became congested with the movements of British motorized units; enemy artillery in the vicinity of Zubza and Jotsoma was considerably increased; the bombardment of the troops occupying Kohima became more and more intense and interdiction fire was persistently directed at supply routes.

Units Ordered to Imphal

About 19 April, the Division received orders from the 15th Army to send a force of three infantry battalions and one artillery battalion under the command of Maj. Gen. Miyazaki toward Imphal. The Division commander realized that, with the transfer of such a large proportion of his strength, the Division would be forced to abandon its offensive tactics. His only alternative was to maintain defensive positions in the vicinity of Kohima in an attempt to block any enemy efforts to reach Imphal. Accordingly, on 20 April he redesignated certain of his assault units as defense units and directed the following dispositions:

    1. The 124th Infantry Regiment (less the 3d Battalion and the 1st and 5th Companies); the 1st Battalion, 138th Infantry Regiment and the 3d Battalion, 31st Mountain Artillery Regiment to assemble in the region southeast of Aradura to prepare for movement toward Imphal.

    2. The Right Defense Unit, composed of the 138th Infantry Regiment (less the 1st Battalion and the 9th Company); the 1st Battalion, 31st Mountain Artillery; one engineer platoon and one medical company to take up positions in the vicinity of Merema.

    3. The Center Defense Unit, composed of the 31st Mountain Artillery Regimental Headquarters; the 3d Battalion, 124th Infantry Regiment (less the 10th Company) and one engineer platoon to defend Kohima.

    4. The Left Assault Unit, with the 58th Infantry as a nucleus, to continue its attacks on Garrison Hill.

On the following day, however, General Sato reconsidered his decision and determined to occupy Garrison Hill prior to complying with the Army directive. The Left Assault Unit was strengthened by the attachment of the 1st Battalion, 138th Infantry Regiment and on the night of 23 April, an all-out attack by the Left Assault Unit was made on Garrison Hill. As in the past, the defenders held fast and inflicted extremely heavy casualties on the attackers, four companies being virtually annihilated. At this point the Division commander realized that if three battalions were to be diverted to Imphal, the 31st Division might be unable to accomplish its primary mission of holding Kohima and preventing enemy reinforcement of

Imphal from the north. Consequently, he decided to disregard the orders of the 15th Army and no troops were moved to Imphal.

Assumption of the Defensive

The 124th Infantry Regiment, assembled near Aradura, was now directed to protect the left flank of the Division and to construct secondary defense positions in the vicinity of Aradura.

The attacks on Garrison Hill were suspended toward the end of April and the Left Assault Unit, redesignated as the Left Defense Unit, was ordered to hold in its present positions.

The 33d Division - May and June

Operations Against Bishenpur (Map No. 17)

As the 33d Division moved north, the Left and Center Assault Units were merged under control of the Division commander. In late April, General Mutaguchi determined to form the axis of the Army offensive along the Bishenpur-Imphal Road to fully exploit the progress of the 33d Division. In early May he directed reinforcement of the Division.[2]

The 33d Division, determined to take Bishenpur before moving against Imphal, prepared the following general plan:

> 1. Prior to the commencement of the general attack, the 215th Infantry Regiment and the 1st Battalion, 214th Infantry Regiment, will occupy the Ngarangial positions now held by the enemy.

---

[2] Reinforcing units were: the 14th Tank Regt; 2d Bn (less 4th Btry), 18th Hvy Fld Arty and 1st AT-Gun Bn from the Yamamoto Detachment and the 1st Bn (less 3d Co), 67th Inf Regt; 2d Bn, 154th Inf Regt and the 151st Inf Regt (less 1st Bn) from Army rear units.

MAP NO. 17

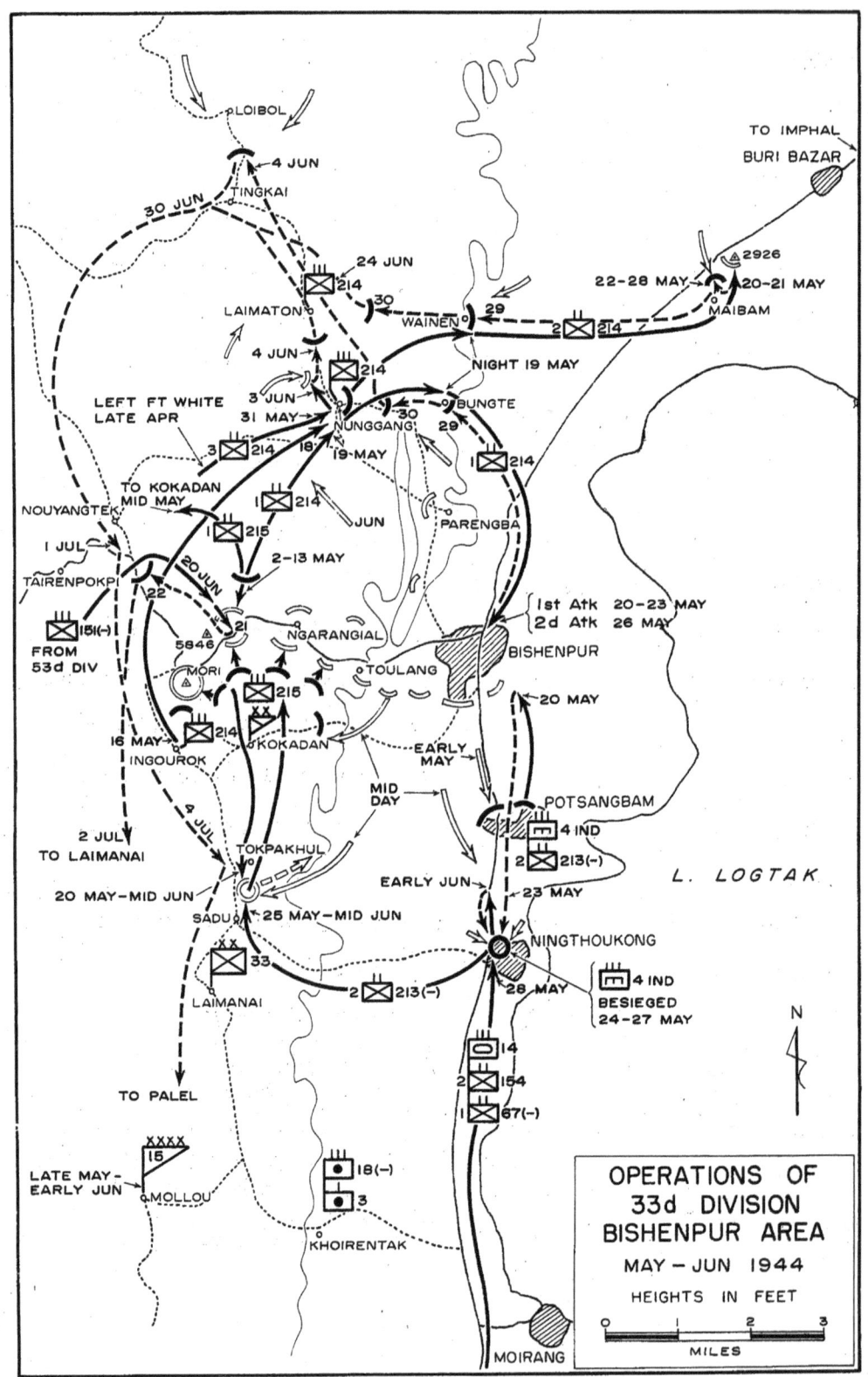

OPERATIONS OF
33d DIVISION
BISHENPUR AREA
MAY – JUN 1944
HEIGHTS IN FEET

2. The 214th Infantry Regiment will complete preparations at Nunggang by 15 May.

3. The attack on Bishenpur will be launched when reinforcements arrive. The 214th Infantry will attack from the north, the 215th Infantry from the west, and all other units from the south.

Attacks began in early May against positions between Hill 5846 and Ngarangial, with two battalions attacking from the north and one from the south. The enemy, in strong positions, withstood a series of attacks which continued until the middle of May.

Meanwhile, the British 5th Division had been flown from Chittagong to the Imphal front and by the middle of May the enemy had sufficient strength in the Imphal area to be capable of launching a large scale attack against the entire 33d Division front.

The Torbung Roadblock (Map No. 14)

As the first step in their offensive, the enemy advanced from the vicinity of Palel and established a roadblock near Torbung on 17 May. Having cut the 33d Division's line of communications, counterattacks were conducted against Sadu, Kokodan and Potsangbam and the 33d Division found itself under attack from all sides.

In the Torbung sector, Lt. Col. Matsuki, CO, 33d Supply Regiment, was given the mission of reopening the line of communications using whatever troops were available in the immediate area. A composite company from the 33d Supply Regiment, which had been deployed in the mountainous area west of Churachandpur, held Hill 4358 against several enemy attacks. On the night of 17 May, approximately 100 men were gathered from rear elements to make the first attack on the roadblock. The attacking group was mounted on trucks and the leaders miscalculating the location of the enemy position drove squarely up to the roadblock and the entire attacking unit was virtually annihilated.

Reinforcements intended for employment in the main front were brought into action to knock out the roadblock and restore the line of communications. The 1st Battalion, 67th Infantry Regiment made attacks on the 19th and 20th of May, suffering tremendous losses. The 2d Battalion, 154th Infantry Regiment and a composite company from the 14th Tank Regiment attacked on the 21st and again on the 23d but were not only unsuccessful in dislodging the enemy, but also suffered extremely heavy losses.

At the same time, the battle situation was becoming more serious in the sector between Laimanai and Kokadan. The enemy had captured a hill known to the Japanese as Mitsukobu Hill, between Sadu and Tokpakhul, endangering Division headquarters at Laimanai. The 215th Infantry Regiment was forced to turn back from its attack on positions west of Ngarangial to secure the Division center.

Division Commander Relieved

In the midst of the 33d Division's difficulties, orders from the 15th Army, dated 15 May, relieved Maj. Gen. Yanagida of command of the Division, effective 24 May. The command was given to Maj. Gen. (later Lt. Gen.) Nobuo Tanaka who arrived at Churachandpur on 18 May. At this time the 15th Army was attempting to move its command post from Indainggyi to Mollou but because of the Torbung roadblock the movement was halted as was General Tanaka's advance to join the Division.

Attack on Bishenpur Renewed

The proposed general attack by the 33d Division was abandoned but the occupation of Bishenpur was still considered essential. The 214th Infantry Regiment was ordered to attack Bishenpur from the north in coordination with an attack launched from the south by the 2d Battalion of the 213th Infantry.

On the night of 19 May the 1st Battalion of the 214th Infantry Regiment left Bungte and attacked Bishenpur at 0200 hours on the 20th, seizing the road fork in the northern sector. Early on 26 May the last charge on Bishenpur was launched by a composite company but it ended when the unit commander, Capt. Moriyama, was killed just as the attackers reached enemy headquarters.

Also on the 20th, the 2d Battalion of the 214th left Wainen and attacked Hill 2926, being checked just below the crest. After daybreak both battalions were exposed to heavy counterattacks and on 22 May, Regimental headquarters lost contact with both battalions, except for occasional sounds of battle. On 27 May, Col. Sakuma, CO, 214th Infantry Regiment, received word the 2d Battalion was still fighting although besieged by the enemy at Maibam.

Col. Sakuma determined to extricate his battalions. On 29 May, the 1st Battalion withdrew to Bungte and the 2d To Wainen. Subsequently both battalions moved about one mile to the west where defense positions were established. As a result of the attacks, only 17 men remained out of 380 in the 1st Battalion while some 37 men out of 540 remained fit for combat in the 2d Battalion. The 3d Battalion (less two companies) arrived at Nunggang from Fort White on 31 May, about two weeks late to engage in the attacks. The Battalion commander was relieved upon arrival, being charged with deliberately delaying the arrival of his unit.

On 20 May, the 2d Battalion of the 213th Infantry Regiment left Potsangbam and attacked Bishenpur from the southeast in concert with the 214th Infantry's attack from the north. Far from achieving any measure of success, the unit was thrown back and, pursued by the enemy, was forced to abandon Potsangbam and withdrew to Ningthoukong about the 23d of May. Furthermore, as the Battalion was almost immediately diverted to reinforce units attacking Mitsukobu Hill, the 4th Independent Engineer Regiment found itself besieged at Ningthoukong on May 24th.

Meanwhile, severe fighting was developing around Mitsukobu Hill and in the area where the 215th Infantry Regiment was making a stand before Ngarangial. Division headquarters was enveloped in the battle line and although the 2d Battalion of the 213th Infantry was thrown into the attack on 25 May, the situation did not improve.

With the Division heavily involved in attempting to eliminate the Torbung roadblock, trying to contain the enemy at Ngarangial and attacking at Mitsukobu Hill, it was forced to leave the 214th Infantry Regiment, north of Bishenpur, to extricate itself as best it could.

Enemy Withdrawal from Torbung

With every unit of the Division hard pressed, on 23 May the enemy suddenly withdrew from the Torbung roadblock toward Bishenpur, a most fortunate development for the 33d Division. Had the roadblock been held only a few days longer, the 33d would have been in serious straits regarding supply and in a most difficult tactical position. The line of communications was, however, reopened on 24 May and the 14th Tank Regiment, the 2d Battalion of the 154th Infantry Regiment and the 1st Battalion of the 67th Infantry Regiment passed through the defile and relieved the 4th Independent Engineer Regiment besieged at Ningthoukong on 28 May.

Change in Balance of Power

The balance of power had shifted very definitely to the enemy and only the indomitable spirit of the 33d Division enabled it to stave off defeat in early June. Between the 8th and 12th of the month a number of attacks were launched in the Ningthoukong area with the expectation that the Tank Regiment would be capable of overcoming all enemy resistance. The Japanese tanks, it developed, were no match for the enemy's M-4 Tanks and with troop strength reduced to about one-half, the defense of Ningthoukong was of the limit of the capabilities of the troops in that sector.

In mid-June the enemy withdrew from Mitsukobu Hill and the center of action once more shifted to the Kokadan-Nagarangial sector. By that time, however, the 215th Infantry (with the 2d Battalion, 213th Infantry attached) was so reduced in strength that it was no longer capable of mounting an effective attack. About the 19th of June, the 151st Infantry Regiment (53d Division) arrived at the front with its leading element of about 300 men. Without waiting for the balance of the regiment to concentrate in the area, the advance element was ordered to attack the north side of Hill 5846. On 21 June the troops of the 151st occupied the hill positions which had so successfully defied the efforts of the 33d Division troops. On the following day, however, the Regiment was hit by strong counterattacking forces and was forced to withdraw to Nouyangtek.

Suspension of the Offensive

In the Nunggang sector, the enemy had enveloped the 214th Infantry Regiment and had taken the hill just north of Nunggang on June 2d. On the same day, the 3d Battalion moved north of Tingkai to protect the right flank of the Regiment and Regimental headquarters withdrew to Laimaton. Isolated, the 214th fought on in the vicinity of Laimaton until the end of June. Movements of enemy units indicated that it was the intention of the enemy to cut off the only possible route of retreat at Tairenpokpi. Becoming cognizant of this possible maneuver, the Division commander directed the 214th Infantry Regiment to withdraw on 29 June. This withdrawal order was the first positive indication of the Division's intention to abandon the offensive against Bishenpur.

On 1 July the 214th Infantry, with only 400 effectives remaining, completed its withdrawal to the area south of Nouyangtek and the 151st was directed to move back to Laimanai. Having been decimated by sickness and straggling en route to the front, the strength of the entire 151st Infantry Regiment was, at that time, less than 100 men.

The Division, with its strength so greatly depleted, was forced to give up mass attacks and to adopt infiltration and guerrilla tactics hoping to exhaust the enemy by gradual attrition. Although these tactics succeeded in inflicting considerable losses on enemy tanks and artillery, it was obvious that the main issue of the campaign had already been settled in favor of the enemy.

15th Division (May and June) (Map No. 18)

In late April the situation of the 15th Division had begun to deterioriate. The Right and Center Assault Units, the major portion of the Division, were compelled to revert exclusively to defense and both units were hard-pressed by the enemy. The British main drive which had first been directed along the Imphal-Ukhrul Road was shifted to the Imphal-Kohima Road. Air attacks were conducted daily and repeated ground attacks were strongly supported by tanks and artillery.

MAP NO. 18

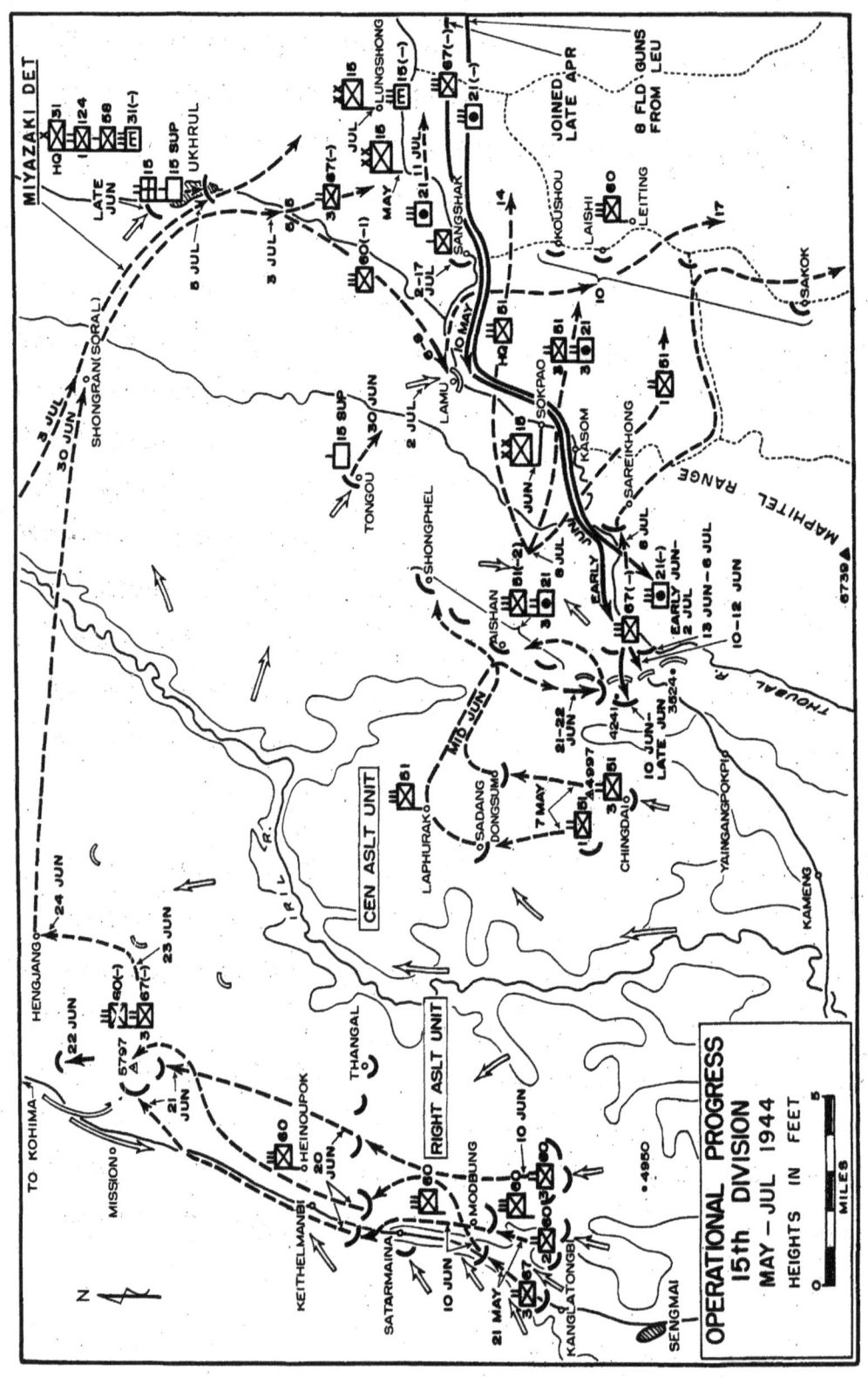

Realizing the vital need for artillery support, in the latter part of April, the Division took steps to have as many as possible of the field guns, that had been left east of the Chindwin River, brought up to the front. In addition, the Headquarters and 2d Battalion of the 67th Infantry Regiment, an Army reserve force, was ordered to join the 15th Division. This unit advanced to Sangshak in early May and seized Lamu on the 10th to secure the rear of the Division.

Enemy Infiltration Tactics

The Right Assault Unit, defending the area north of Kanglatongbi, and the Center Assault Unit, between Sadang and Dongsum, withstood repeated attacks through the month of May. During May, enemy forces began infiltrating through the wide gap between the Right and Center Assault Units and other enemy units were parachuted into the rear of the Division positions. These tactics were successful in isolating the Japanese positions and supply lines were cut. It became increasingly difficult to obtain provisions locally and neither assault unit received any supplies from the rear supply installations. The Right Assault Unit dispatched parties as far as the area west of the Imphal Plain in efforts to obtain food. The Center Unit was successful in capturing some quantities of enemy supplies but many of the more isolated units received nothing and, on occasion, were forced to exist on roots and grasses for periods of a week or more.

Attempts to Consolidate Positions

In early June, 21st Field Artillery Regiment arrived at Division headquarters, in Sokpao, bringing eight field pieces with 27 rounds of ammunition per weapon. On 10 June the Division ordered the 67th Infantry to attack enemy positions on Hills 4241 and 3524. The unit succeeded in occupying the former objective but failed in its efforts to take Hill 3524. The Division then determined to utilize the Center Assault Unit in an attempt to penetrate the pass adjacent to Hill 3524. The Center Assault Unit moved back to Aishan and on 21 - 22 June attacked enemy positions north of Hill 4241 with the 1st Battalion of the 51st Infantry Regiment. The attack was only partially successful and the Battalion drew back to Aishan.

Meanwhile the Right Assault Unit was battling desperately to prevent the enemy from re-opening the Imphal-Kohima highway. All its heavy weapons, except one machine gun, had been destroyed and June 21st found the Unit making a last ditch stand on the main road near Hill 5797, east of Mission.

Retreat of the 31st Division

The 31st Division, which had been executing an unauthorized withdrawal from Kohima, had completely deserted the Kohima area by 20 June and fled toward Ukhrul. The retreat of the 31st Division released strong enemy forces which suddenly appeared on the front of the Right Assault Unit and pushed through to open the Imphal-Kohima Road, which had been successfully blockaded for 80 days.

The 15th Division was now faced with the decision of whether to follow the example of the 31st and withdraw without permission or to hold to the last. Although there was some dissension among the members of the Division staff, the final decision was to follow the latter course and defend its positions as long as possible. In spite of the fact that the maintenance of its present defenses represented the maximum capability of the Division, the 15th Army now urged the Division to retake Mission and rush toward Imphal. The 15th Division, however, determined that the most pressing problem was the relief of the Right Assault Unit, which was cut off from the rest of the Division. The Unit was directed to join the Miyazaki Detachment, rear guard of the 31st Division, and withdraw in the direction of Ukhrul on 22 June. The main force of the Division then went into defense positions in a line extending generally from Ukhrul through Tongou, Shongphel and Aishan to the 3524 Pass in order to be in position to cover and pick up the Right Assault Unit and the Miyazaki Detachment as they withdrew to the east. In order to hold the new defense positions, all available men, including all those in the rear service units, were thrown into the line.

Withdrawal to Sangshak Area

On 2 July, Division headquarters and units under its direct control, moved back from Sokpao to the area east of Sangshak. The enemy immediately occupied Lamu with a force that had advanced via Tongou.

On the following day, Lt. Gen. Uichi Shibata arrived at Lungshong to take command of the Division and Division headquarters was established there. Lt. Gen. Yamanouchi, who had been relieved from duty effective 15 May, was carried from the battlefield on a litter and later died in a hospital at Maymyo.

The Right Assault Unit arrived south of Ukhrul on 3 July and its task force organization was dissolved. The Miyazaki Detachment arrived in Ukhrul on the 5th and was placed under the 15th Division.

On 5 July the Division was ordered by the 15th Army to take the offensive and drive toward Imphal along the Thoubal River. Although painfully aware of its inability to launch an offensive, under the pretext of preparing for the operation, the 15th Division recalled the 51st and 67th Infantry Regiments, which were holding the southwestern portion of the defense line, in the area west of Kasom. To re-open a route for their withdrawal, the 60th Infantry Regiment was directed to drive the enemy from Lamu. Attacks were launched but the Regiment was so low in strength that its attacks were ineffective and the enemy continued to occupy Lamu. The 67th Infantry Regiment had been ordered to cover the retreat of the Center Assault Unit, but it withdrew so early and precipitously from the vicinity of Sareikhong that the balance of the Unit (principally the 51st Infantry Regiment and the 3d Battalion, 21st Field Artillery Regiment) was encircled.

Col. Omoto, the commander of the unit, notified Division headquarters that he planned to penetrate the encirclement in three columns on the night of 8 July. In order to cover and pick up the units which might succeed in the breakthrough, on 10 July the 60th Infantry took up positions along a line running from Sangshak to Sakok, via Koushou, Laishi and Leiting.

Offensive Abandoned

On or about the 10th of July the Division received its first defense orders from 15th Army: To establish a defensive line from Lungshong through Sangshak to Maphitel Hill. This disposition was advantageous to the Division in that it would permit redeployment of its main force in the area east of Lungshong, Sangshak and Sakok where it would be under tighter control.

31st Division May and June (Map No. 19)

As a result of the repeated assaults carried out during April the 31st Division had suffered extensive casualties and neither supplies nor reinforcements had been received from the rear. Only a very small amount of ammunition remained, reserves of provisions as well as forage were dangerously low, and local stocks of food were practically exhausted. The Division was, in fact, rapidly losing its offensive ability. On the other hand, in early May, the British received reinforcements and turned to the offensive.

MAP NO. 19

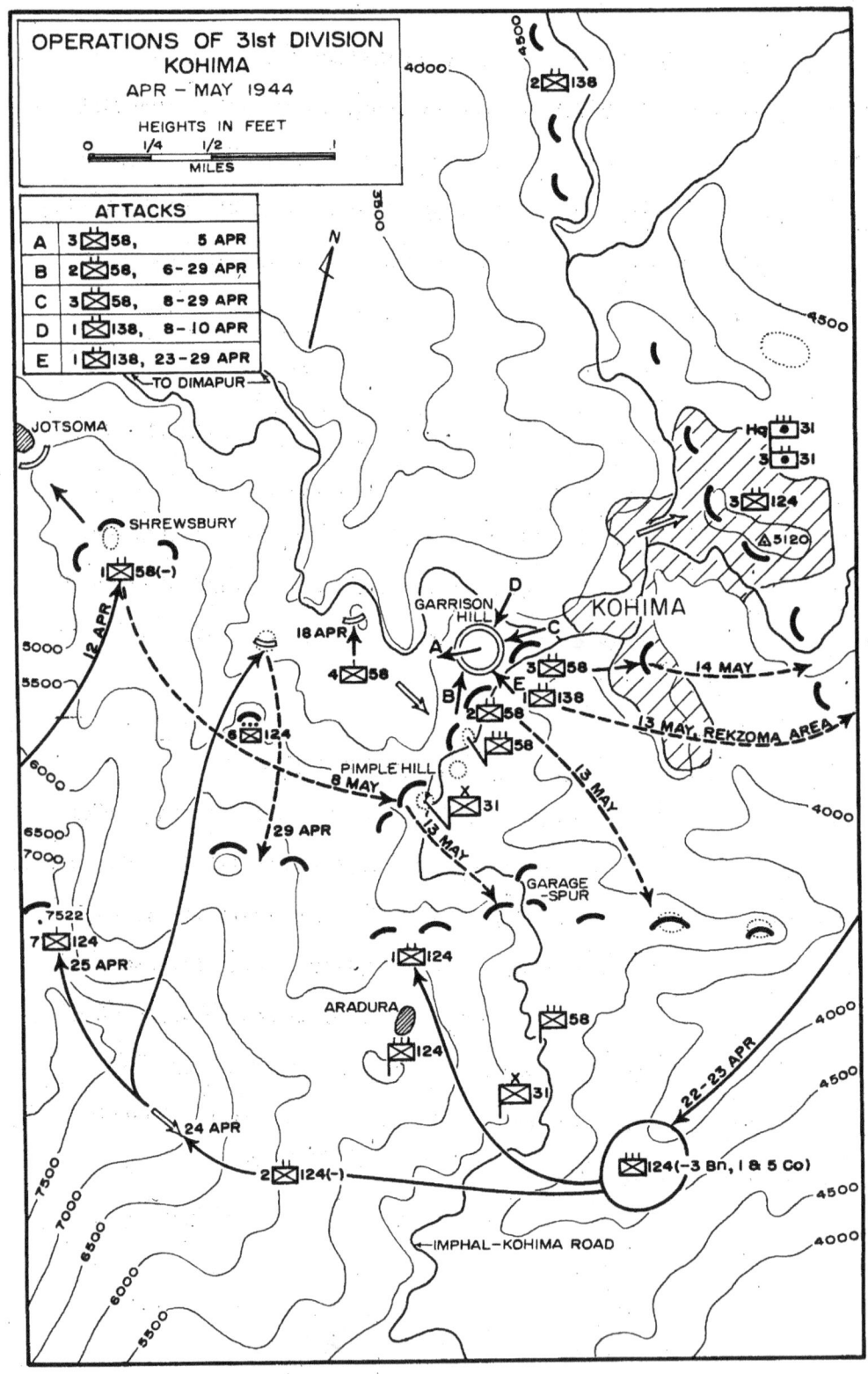

General Offensive by the Enemy

The first enemy attack was directed against the Left Defense Unit in position southwest of Kohima. The attack, which followed a one hour artillery preparation by an estimated 100 guns, was led by a mass of tanks. This first attack was repulsed but at a frightful cost. The enemy followed with second and third attacks which resulted in isolating the three defense units from each other. Although strong pressure was maintained against all defense units, the enemy directed its most intensive efforts against the Left Defense Unit.

General Miyazaki took direct command of his Left Defense Unit, fighting in the forefront at Pimple Hill despite the Division commander's pleas to move to the rear. The 1st Battalion, 58th Infantry Regiment was pulled back from Shrewsbury to Pimple Hill during the night of 7 May. The Division commander ordered the Left Defense Unit to withdraw to the secondary defense line north of Aradura on 13 May and at the same time placed the 124th Infantry Regiment (less the 3d Battalion) under General Miyazaki. The 3d Battalion, 58th Infantry Regiment was transferred to the Center Defense Unit to defend southern Kohima and the 1st Battalion, 138th Infantry Regiment was assigned to protect the right flank of the Division in the sector of Rekzoma.

Following the attacks on the Left Defense Unit, the enemy directed a vigorous attack toward Hill 5120. Heavy fighting developed at the top of the hill and although the 3d Battalion of the 124th Infantry Regiment maintained its hold, the enemy continued its pressure.

In the Cheswema-Merema area, enemy pressure was comparatively light and the Right Defense Unit had little trouble in holding its positions.

In late May the lack of ammunition as well as provisions and forage, coupled with the decrease in combat potential made it increasingly difficult to hold the defense positions. An element of the British force had infiltrated from the north through the right flank of the Division and posed a threat to the line of communications. The guard unit of Division Headquarters and other rear units were assigned the task of clearing out the infiltrating enemy but found it extremely difficult to locate and mop-up this constantly growing force.

Decision to Withdraw

In the meantime, the rainy season had started and the swelling of streams and the bombing of bridges by enemy aircraft caused the complete disruption of vehicular traffic. The Division commander repeatedly requested supplies from the Army but the supply system was disrupted. Late in May the Division notified 15th Army that it was planning to withdraw to a position which would enable it to receive supplies.

The Army commander replied that it was most inadvisable for the Division to withdraw at this critical time when the fall of Imphal was imminent and ordered the Division to hold Kohima at all costs. At this time the 15th Army still thought that the capture of Imphal was possible and that with the occupation of that city, the 31st Division would be extricated from its difficulties. In spite of the orders of the Army commander and the importance of holding at Kohima, Lt. Gen. Sato, the Division commander, arbitrarily abandoned Kohima and began retreating with his Division on 31 May.

To cover the retreat of the Division and to deny the Imphal-Kohima Road to the enemy for the longest possible time, the Miyazaki Detachment was reorganized with the 31st Infantry Group Headquarters; the 1st Battalion, 124th Infantry Regiment; the 1st Company, 58th Infantry Regiment and the main body of the 31st Engineer Regiment; a total strength of approximately 600 men. The Detachment withdrew from Aradura on the night of 4 June, conducting delaying actions from 5 to 12 June at Viswema, from 14 to 16 June at Maosongsang and from 18 to 20 June at Maram. The enemy finally broke up the rear guard action of the Miyazaki at Maram at 1600 hours, 20 June and the Detachment withdrew east toward Ukhrul.

Operations Against the Wingate Airborne Force

Maj. Gen. Hayashi being given the mission to take over operations against the Wingate Brigade, partially relieved the pressure on the 15th Army for the elimination of this threat and it was able to concentrate greater attention on the Imphal Operation.

On 26 March, the 2d Battalion, 29th Infantry Regiment, engaged the British 16th Brigade near Lake Indaw. The enemy brigade, which had advanced through the jungle from Ledo was thought at that time to be a part of the airborne force. Before the enemy was driven back, after a five day engagement, four battalions (the 2d Battalion, 29th Infantry Regiment; 2d Battalion, 51st Infantry Regiment; 3d Battalion, 114th Infantry Regiment and the 141st Battalion, 24th Mixed Brigade) had been thrown into the battle. (Map No. 20).

From 6 to 17 April, General Hayashi conducted repeated attacks on the Mawlu perimeter but the strong, closely integrated honeycomb defenses withstood even the most desperate efforts of the Japanese units. In the meantime an enemy group had cut the highway at Tonlon. The Hayashi Unit withdrew from Mawlu and drove off the group at Tonlon on the 25th and 26th of April. The Hayashi Unit then moved to Indaw to reorganize and prepare for further operations.

MAP NO. 20

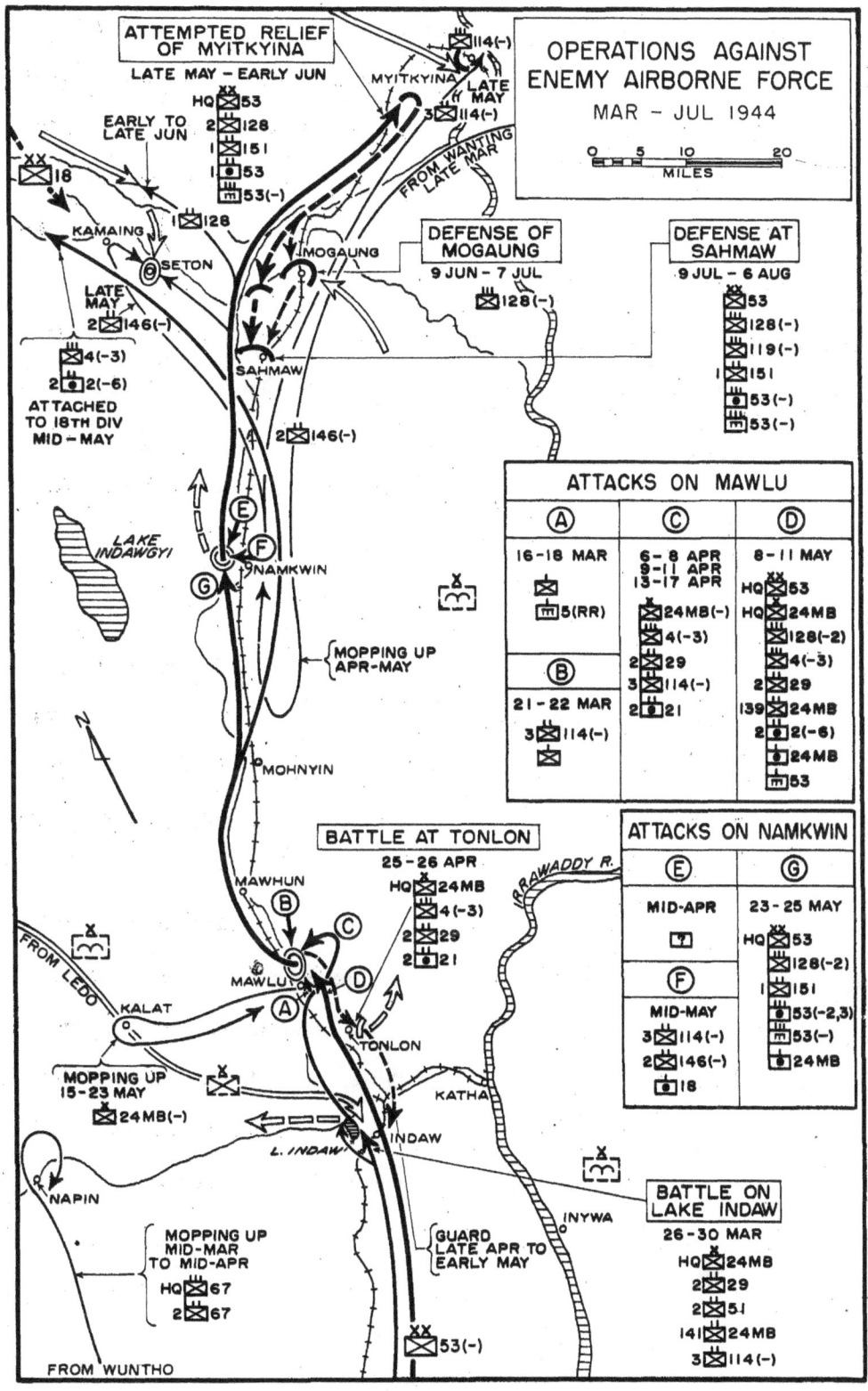

During the time in which the Unit was reorganizing, a strong enemy force built defense positions on a hill west of Namkwin. This perimeter defense also proved extremely effective and withstood repeated attacks by the 2d Battalion, 146th Infantry Regiment, the 3d Battalion, 114th Infantry Regiment and the rear service units of the 18th Division.

In a surprise move Merrill's Marauders of the Stilwell forces seized the airstrip at Myitkyina on 17 May and the 3d Battalion of the 114th Infantry was ordered to reinforce the units at Myitkyina. The enemy group at Namkwin was left in control of the sector unitl such time as the 53d Division could be brought up from the south.

Activation of the 33d Army

As the airborne raid developed into a large scale operation, the possibility of a coordinated offensive with assistance from the outside became a strong possibility. As a direct consequence, the formation of the long planned 33d Army was accelerated, with organization orders being issued on 8 April.

In late April, a threefold mission was established for the newly formed Army: To take charge of operations against the Stilwell Force, advancing from the north, along the Hukawng Valley; the Y-Force coming from Yunnan Province in China; and the Wingate Airborne Force, operating in Mawlu-Myitkyina area. Included in the order of battle of the 33d Army were the 18th and 56th Divisions as well as the 24th Mixed Brigade and other units presently engaged against the Wingate Force. The 53d Division, which was en route to Northern Burma from Malaya, was placed under the 33d Army on 24 April.

Employment of the 53d Division

The 53d Division, transferred from Japan to act as a strategic reserve for the Southern Army, had arrived at Saigon and Singapore in four echelons between January and April 1944. The Burma Area Army had contemplated the employment of the Division in the southwest coastal area but, in view of the threat posed by the Wingate invasion, determined to use the 53d in northern Burma. On 27 March, the Division was ordered to Burma. On 4 May, the Division advanced to the vicinity of Indaw and all units in that area were placed under its command. However, the 53d Reconnaissance Regiment, the 1st Battalion of the 119th Infantry Regiment and the 2d Battalion of the 128th Infantry Regiment had been detached from the 53d and attached to the 56th Division in the Lashio area. The 151st Infantry Regiment (less the 1st Battalion), on arriving in the vicinity of Mawlu, was assigned to the 33d Division. Since the 119th Infantry Regiment was still en route, the actual strength of the Division, when its headquarters was established in the vicinity of Indaw, was only the 128th Infantry Regiment (less the 2d Battalion) and the 1st Artillery Battalion.

The 53d Division and its attached units was preparing to launch an attack against Mawlu on 11 May but, before preparations could be completed, the enemy in that area withdrew to the north.

Immediately following the enemy's withdrawal from Mawlu the 33d Army made the following disposition of strength: the 53d Division to attack Namkwin and then reinforce the 18th Division; the 4th Infantry Regiment (less the 3d Battalion) to advance to the Hukawng Valley; the 24th Mixed Brigade to mop-up in the Kalat area; the 2d Battalion, 29th Infantry Regiment to be transferred to the 56th Division and the 2d Battalion, 128th Infantry Regiment to revert to the 53d Division.

The 53d Division attacked the enemy defense perimeter near Namkwin on the 23d of May and on the 25th succeeded in driving the defenders from their positions. The Division, having received a change of orders, instead of reinforcing the 18th Division, advanced toward Myitkyina. The 53d Division arrived in the sector west of Myitkyina about the end of May and prepared to relieve the besieged Myitkyina Garrison.

Meanwhile the 18th Division had been driven into a corner in the Kamaing area. In early June, therefore, the 53d Division was again required to turn back to Mogaung and cover the retreat of the 18th Division. At the same time, Mogaung was under attack by elements of Wingate's Airborne Force and its situation had become critical. The 1st Battalion and the 10th Company of the 128th Infantry

Regiment were annihilated in a sharp engagement on the north bank of the Mogaung River and the main body of the 128th fought on in the vicinity of Mogaung until 7 July. The efforts of the 53d Division enabled the 18th Division to withdraw from Kamaing, whereupon the 53d established positions on the Sahmaw River and operations against the Wingate Airborne Force came to an end.

Results of Wingate Invasion

The penetration of the airborne force into northern Burma resulted in the upsetting of the 15th Army's timetable which had contemplated the completion of the Imphal Operation before the enemy could launch an offensive against Burma. The raiding force greatly affected Army operations and eventually led to the total abandonment of northern Burma.

The immediate effects of the airborne landings on the Imphal operation were:

> 1. The 15th Army was unable to advance its headquarters toward Imphal until late April, due to the necessity of directing measures being taken to contain the airborne invasion. As a consequence, liaison with the divisions involved in the Imphal Operation was inadequate and resulted in alienating the division commanders from the Army headquarters.
>
> 2. Transportation of supplies to units engaged in the Imphal Operations became very difficult because the airborne force not only cut off the lines of communication for the 15th and 31st Divisions, but prevented the scheduled transfer of vehicles from the Indaw-Homalin area south to the Shwebo-Kalewa Road.

3. Elements of the 15th Division were diverted from the Imphal Operation and the 53d Division, the only reserve force available to the Area Army, was involved in combatting the Wingate forces and could not be used as a strategic reserve for the Imphal Operation.

4. The 5th Air Division was forced to operate against the enemy airborne units to a considerable extent and was not able to render the fullest possible support to the Imphal Operation.

The airborne invasion also cut the supply route of the 18th Division which was already heavily involved in fighting in the Hukawng area and compounded the increasingly difficult position of that division.

On the other hand, because the enemy air power was absorbed in supporting the Wingate airborne landings, the crossing of the Chindwin River, in the initial phase of the Imphal offensive, was accomplished without enemy air interference.

Withdrawal from Imphal

Redisposition of the 15th Army (General Reference Map I)

Late in May the 15th Army commander estimated that, since the situation on the 33d Division front south of Imphal was about to become a stalemate, it would be useless to attempt to develop the battle situation further in that area. The situation of the 15th Division north of Imphal was similarly hopeless. The only alternative was to withdraw from the Imphal area and move against Palel. However, by the end of May the plan for the redisposition of the Army had not yet been completed. The Army staff had suggested the employment of the 31st Division in the area between the 15th Division and the Yamamoto Detachment of the 33d Division but before this disposition could be thoroughly studied, the 31st Division began its unauthorized retreat.

Although the retreat of the 31st Division was clearly a serious breach of military discipline the Army commander determined to use it to good advantage. Inasmuch as it was desired to save something from the present debacle by conducting a last successful offensive, he temporarily approved the retreat of the 31st Division, terming it a withdrawal movement in preparation for the offensive on Palel.

The Palel Offensive

The Army commander left Mollou on 3 June and met Lt. Gen. Kawabe, CG, Burma Area Army, on 5 June at Indainggyi. General Kawabe had come to the front to view the situation first hand and to get General Mutaguchi's honest opinion of operational prospects. Both generals eventually agreed that the offensive on Palel offered a last hope to salvage some advantage from the Imphal Operation. About 7 June the Army Command Post was moved from Indainggyi to Kuntang to direct the battle from a position in the rear of the Yamamoto Detachment.

The 1st Battalion, 213th Infantry Regiment which left Akyab to rejoin the Army on 1 June and the 61st Infantry Regiment (less the 2d Battalion, plus one battery of the 4th Artillery Regiment) which had been ordered to the 15th Army from Sumatra in mid-May, were expected to reinforce the Yamamoto Detachment but were long delayed in reaching the front.

Rallying the exhausted troops of his command, Maj. Gen. Yamamoto ordered the Nukui Unit to make a surprise raid on Palel. The Nukui Unit, composed of the 213th Infantry Regiment Headquarters; the 1st Battalion, 60th Infantry Regiment; the 2d Battalion, 51st Infantry Regiment and other supporting units left Tengnoupal on 13 June and after repulsing an enemy attack near Langgol, advanced to the hill northeast of Palel. The engagement at Langgol had however, apprised the enemy of the presence of the raiding group and a surprise attack was no longer possible. The Nukui Unit then moved back to Khudai-Khunou from which location two raiding parties were dispatched on 1 July. These raiding parties penetrated the Palel defenses and damaged the airfield and some barracks buildings.

Meanwhile the 31st Division was continuing its retreat from Kohima. Stretcher cases totalled about 1,500 and much of the remaining manpower of the Division was required to carry them. Those who were not employed as stretcher-bearers were utilized in hauling artillery pieces and other heavy weapons since almost all the horses were now dead. The rainy season made movement much more difficult and drained the waning strength of the men.

On 4 June the Division received orders to attack Imphal but the retreat toward Humine along the Kohima-Ukhrul-Humine Road continued. On the 19th of June the Chief of Staff of the 15th Army met Lt. Gen. Sato the commander of the 31st Division, at Lungshong and ordered him to stop the retreat and rejoin the battle south of the 15th Division. The 31st Division commander argued that 15th Army's failure to provide his division with supplies made it impossible for him to comply with the order and continued his withdrawal.

The action of the 31st Division not only destroyed all hope of taking Imphal but also placed the 15th Division in a very vulnerable position. The situation for that Division grew graver when the enemy attacked after breaking through the Miyazaki rear guard defense on the Kohima-Imphal Road on 20 June. The Army commander requested higher authorities to discipline and replace Lt. Gen. Sato and at the end of June, Lt. Gen. Miyazaki (promoted from Maj. Gen. on 27 June) was given temporary command of the 31st Division.

The over-all situation of the 15th Army went from bad to worse and the only hope remaining was to rally the 31st at Humine, give the troops a few days rest and then, after a reorganization, to dispatch them to the northern flank of the Yamamoto Detachment to capture Palel. In early July the 31st Division was concentrated in the area east of Myothit but discipline had disintegrated to the point that the Division could scarcely be termed a combat force. The Torikai Unit was organized with the 138th Infantry Regiment (less one battalion); the 2d Battalion, 124th Infantry Regiment and one artillery battalion to reinforce the Yamamoto Detachment. At the same time, the 15th Army ordered the 33d Division to attack Palel from the south with the 214th Infantry Regiment. The newly formed Torikai Unit, however, failed to join the Yamamoto Detachment and the order for the 33d to attack Palel was never carried out.

All hope of capturing Imphal or Palel was now gone and the 15th Army realized that it would be fortunate if it could extricate itself from its extremely hazardous position without greater losses.

CHAPTER 4

WITHDRAWAL FROM EASTERN INDIA

Suspension of the Imphal Operation

As early as May, many staff officers of the Burma Area Army, particularly those in charge of supply, began taking a pessimistic view of the U-Go (Imphal) Operation. The Vice-Chief of Staff of IGHQ, Lt. Gen. Hata, visited Rangoon on 2 May to check on the development of the offensive. On his return to Tokyo, he advised General Tojo that the operation had little chance for success. However, at the same time, Lt. Col. Kaizaki of the Southern Army staff wired from the battle-front that some possibility for victory still remained. General Tojo accepted this latter opinion and directed the continuance of the operation. In spite of the pessimistic attitude of many of their staff officers, until late June, Generals Kawabe and Mutaguchi never faltered in their resolution to pursue the Imphal Operation to a successful conclusion. On 20 June, however, when the British broke through the last defenses on the Kohima-Imphal Road, the inevitability of defeat became obvious.

The collapse of the 31st Division, the advent of the rainy season and the suspension of the flow of military supplies forced the 15th Army to abandon all hope of recovering from the disastrous situation. On 26 June the 15th Army commander reported to the Area Army that he considered it necessary to withdraw the Army west to the hill line on the west bank of the Chindwin River, the hills west of Mawlaik and south to the vicinity of Tiddim to build a defensive line along the India-Burma frontier. Since the Area Army had received no orders for a suspension of the operation from the Southern Army, the Area Army urged the 15th Army to continue the offensive.

General Kawabe, however, decided to suggest to the Southern Army that the U-Go Operation be suspended and to this end he dispatched Col. Aoki, of the Area Army staff, to Southern Army Headquarters at Singapore on 29 June. The Army General Staff and the Southern Army immediately approved suspension of the offensive and appropriate orders were issued by Southern Army on 4 July.

On 5 July, the Burma Area Army directed the 15th Army to prepare for withdrawal while continuing its drive toward Palel. Since the offensive plan prepared by the 15th Army was too large in scope, on 9 July the Area Army specified a smaller concept, directing the main force of the Army to immediately withdraw to a line connecting the Zibyu Mountains, Mawlaik, Kalewa and Gangaw.

On 15 July the Army transmitted the necessary orders to the divisions, initiating the following plan of withdrawal (Gen. Ref. Map I):

> 1. Beginning 16 July, the 15th Division will withdraw its main force to Sittaung along the road connecting Ukhrul, Humine, Tamu and Sittaung. Elements of the Division will occupy the crossing point on the Yu River near Yanan as well as key points in the Minthami Range between Yanan and Sittaung in order to check enemy pursuit.

2. The 31st Division will withdraw its main force to the Thaungdut sector via the road connecting Humine and Thaungdut. The Division will dispose rear guard elements at key points along the route of withdrawal to check enemy pursuit.

3. The Yamamoto Detachment will withdraw from its present battle line on 24 July and secure the strategic line connecting Kuntaung and Moreh until 31 July in order to cover the withdrawal of the main force of the Army from the Kabaw Valley. Thereafter, the main force of the Detachment will withdraw to Mawlaik via the road connecting Moreh, Ahlaw and Mawlaik. To cover the withdrawal route of the 33d Division, one element will occupy Yazagyo to check the enemy advancing southward from Shuganu through the Kabaw Valley to Kalemyo.

4. The 33d Division will commence its withdrawal on 17 July. The main force will withdraw to Tiddim through Chikha and Tonzang while an element holds the narrow valley at Torbung.

Withdrawal to the Chindwin River

The 31st Division assembled in the vicinity of Thaungdut in late July but, due to the disintegration of military discipline, failed to conduct the ordered delaying actions along the Thaungdut-Humine line. As a direct consequence the flank and rear of the 15th Division were exposed. The 31st was then ordered to Sittaung. Lt. Gen. Tsuchitaro Kawada arrived at Intabaung on 2 August to take command of the Division. He was successful in rallying the demoralized troops and, with the aid of the 61st Infantry Regiment, the Division stood fast west of Sittaung throughout the month of August. From this position the 31st Division provided cover for the units of the 15th Army which were concentrating in the Sittaung assembly area.

The 15th Division moved southeast to the Kabaw Valley, some units along the road connecting Ukhrul, Sangshak and Humine and others via the steep mountain trail running west of the road. Withdrawing in good order, holding off harassing attacks and successfully by-passing strong enemy units, the Division reached Thaungdut in early August. From the 13th to the 18th of August elements of the Division checked an attack launched by the British-Indian 19th Division in the Minthami Range, west of Thaungdut, although combat strength at that time had reduced all battalions to between 50 and 70 men each.

The Tengnoupal position, held by the Yamamoto Detachment was penetrated from the direction of Sibong by the enemy 20th Division which had advanced to that vicinity prior to the start of the 15th Army withdrawal. The penetration cut the Detachment's route of withdrawal, but the 61st Infantry Regiment (less the 2d Battalion), which had arrived at Tamu on the night of 23 July, immediately counterattacked and reopened the route. The Yamamoto Detachment then withdrew from Tengnoupal on July 24th to positions in the vicinity of Moreh to cover the withdrawal of the main force of the Army. The Detachment was successful in holding back the enemy until the night of 30 July, when the 213th Infantry Regiment pulled back to Mawlaik via Witok and the balance of the Detachment moved to Mawlaik via Sittaung.

Planning to trap the 15th Army west of the Chindwin River, the British launched a daring pursuit along the entire front - relying on air lift for supply. The British-Indian 19th Division attacked in the Sittaung area, the 20th Division along the Yu River and in the Mawlaik sector, the 11th East African Division drove through the Kabaw Valley and the British-Indian 5th Division moved south, covering the Bishenpur-Torbung-Tonzang-Tiddim Road. Before the 15th Army had completed **its** concentration on the west bank of the Chindwin River, the 11th East African Division was approaching the Khamphat River line and pushing on to Yazagyo.

The route of the 15th Army through the area between the Yu and the Chindwin Rivers was marked by the thousands of dead and dying Japanese soldiers who had fallen in the march. The Chindwin River was swollen to a width of 1,000 to 1,500 yards and no river crossing preparations had been possible. There was little food or forage in the designated assembly area west of the Chindwin.

The 33d Division distinguished itself by displaying almost superhuman fighting power and repeatedly launched counterattacks against the pursuing British-Indian 5th Division. The Yamamoto Detachment, however, had failed to cover the Yazagyo area and, in mid-August the 33d Division found itself the vicinity of Chikha facing the serious threat of having its route of withdrawal cut by the enemy which was infiltrating into the Yazagyo area from Moreh and Shuganu through the Kabaw Valley

Withdrawal to the Zibyu Range

Having evacuated its Kuntaung command post on 23 July, Army headquarters established a new command post southeast of Kalewa on 30 July and then moved to Shwebo in mid-August. At that time, the Army commander issued the order to initiate the second phase of the withdrawal which would establish the defense line between the Zibyu Mountain Range and Kalewa. All telecommunications had broken down between Army headquarters and the 15th and 31st Divisions and it took about five days to relay the following withdrawal order:

>   1. The Army will withdraw to the strategic line connecting Indaw, the Zibyu Range, Mawlaik, Kalewa and Gangaw and establish close liaison with the 53d Division (which will hold Pinwe during delaying operations).
>
>   2. The 15th Division will cross the Chindwin River in the vicinity of Thaungdut on 25 August, advance its main force along the Paungbyin-Pinbon-Wuntho Road and a smaller force along the Paungbyin-Pinlebu Road. Keeping close liaison with the left of the 53d Division, the 15th Division will occupy a line along the Zibyu Range west of Pinbon and Pinlebu and destroy the assaulting enemy. One element will be disposed between the Zibyu Range and the Chindwin River to check enemy infiltration.
>
>   3. The 31st Division and the units under direct command of the Army in the Sittaung sector will cross the Chindwin River on 25 August. Part of the Division will move to the Shwebo-Sagaing area via the Pantha-Mutaik-Yeu-Shwebo route while the main force moves via the Paungbyin-Pinlebu-Wuntho-Shwebo Road. The Division will exercise all speed in recovering its fighting strength and will be prepared for the next operation.

4. The 15th and 31st Divisions will dispose powerful units along the west bank of the Chindwin River to act as rear guards covering the river crossing of the main force of the Army. The rear units will withdraw on the night of 30 August.

5. The Army engineer unit will send its main force to the 31st Division and a smaller force to the 15th Division to assist in river crossing operations.

6. Men for hospitalization and heavy weapons will be transported down the Chindwin River to Kalewa by small boats and moved from there to Shwebo or Monywa by motor vehicle or boat.

7. The main force of the Yamamoto Detachment, keeping contact with the left flank of the 15th Division, will hold the area in the vicinity of Mawlaik with a smaller force securing the vicinity of Yazagyo. The Detachment will support the withdrawal of the forces of the 31st and 33d Divisions and will thereafter revert to 33d Division command.

8. The 33d Division will move its main force to the sector around Kalewa and a smaller force to the Gangaw area and will occupy the strategic areas around Mawlaik, Kalewa and Gangaw to destroy the attacking enemy.

The second phase of the withdrawal went generally according to schedule, and the rear guards of the 15th and 31st Divisions crossed to the east bank of the Chindwin River on 30 and 31 August, respectively. At the beginning of the crossing operation, a serious setback was experienced - it had been planned to bring small boats upstream to the crossing area with supplies for the Army and to utilize the same boats to evacuate casualties and heavy weapons south to Kalewa. Because of the enemy air activity over the Chindwin

River, it was impossible to bring the boats to the crossing points. As a result, approximately 3,000 sick and wounded were forced to cross the river and continue to the rear on foot with increasingly heavy death losses.

The 31st Division, due to supply difficulties, changed its plan and withdrew along the Pantha-Mutaik-Yeu Route with its main force reaching Shwebo by the middle of October.

Although the 15th Division was able to withdraw to the designated assembly areas near Pinlebu and Wuntho by the end of September, personnel losses increased during the withdrawal and all members of the Division, including the commanding general, suffered severely due to epidemics and lack of food supplies. Military discipline and morale were lowered to a deplorable state and much equipment, including side arms, was destroyed or abandoned. There were wholesale desertions as men and small units left their parent organizations to search for food. Battalions generally retained only one heavy machine gun, two light machine guns and two grenade launchers - strength averaged 50 men.

Having successfully repulsed the enemy groups which threatened its route of withdrawal, the 33d Division successfully crossed the Manipur River on 12 September and continued toward the Kabaw Valley. The Division maintained strict military discipline and reasonably high morale, conducting the difficult withdrawal from the Imphal plains to Tonzang without discarding equipment. After the 15th of

September the withdrawal became more difficult. The enemy 5th Division, having advanced to the area between Tonzang and Kalemyo, the only route of withdrawal open to the 33d, launched a strong attack, and by September 20th, the 33d Division was pushed back to Tiddim.

The Imphal Operation had not only failed to achieve the objective of establishing a strong defense line to secure Burma and encourage Indian independence, but had resulted in the virtual destruction of the 15th Army. (Chart 3).

Line of Communications

The 15th Army was in serious difficulties as regards transportation. It had lost over 70 per cent of its vehicles, all its horses and oxen. The Myitkyina Railway was usable only for short runs at night and the majority of the boats on the Irrawaddy and Chindwin Rivers had been destroyed.

In the meantime, military supplies for the 15th Army had been accumulated in the rear areas by the Area Army. In the new defense disposition of the 15th Army, supply points were established for the divisions as follows:

     15th Division ..... Wuntho

     31st Division ..... Sagaing and Mandalay

     33d Division ...... Yeu and Kalewa

     53d Division ...... Indaw

CHART 3

Personnel Losses of 15th Army in the
Imphal Operation

	15th Div	31st Div	33d Div	Army Troops	Total
Actual Strength (15 Mar 44)	15,280	15,000*	18,000*	36,000*	84,280
Casualties (30 Sep 44)				8,000*	
KIA	3,678	3,700	5,065		
MIA	747	500*	405		
Deaths from Disease	3,843	2,064	2,500*		
Total	8,268	6,264	7,970	8,000	30,502
Survivors	7,012	8,736	10,030	28,000*	53,778
Hospitalized as of Sep 44	3,703	2,800*	4,500*	12,000*	23,003
Available for duty	3,309	5,936	5,530	16,000	30,775**

* Estimated.

** The great majority of those on duty were sick, suffering from wounds and malnutrition.

The 5th Railway Regiment, the Special Railway Unit, the 45th Independent Motor Transport Battalion, elements of the 73d Line of Communications Sector Unit, the Area Army Supply Depots, and a provisional waterways transport unit were placed under the 15th Army as the area of operations expanded to the rear. These were expected to constitute the main strength of the rear service force, for none of 15th Army logistical units, particularly the transport services, had fully recovered from the Imphal Operation. In late September the Army started systematic logistic activities in support of the withdrawal operation.

Large-scale enemy airborne operations in the Army's rear area were expected as was infiltration along the extensive front. Because of this anticipated activity, it was necessary to evacuate the munitions which had been accumulated northwest of the Irrawaddy River and to disperse them behind the defense lines.

In the logistic plan for the withdrawal operation and subsequent defensive operation, special importance was attached to the delivery as well as the evacuation of military supplies. The amount of ammunition, ordnance and medical supplies in areas northwest of the Irrawaddy would be limited to that needed to actually replace the materiel expended by each force. Only the fuel required for the withdrawal of rear elements and for the division's operations would be kept on hand. Approximately one month's supply of provisions and forage for each force would be accumulated by the divisions and the most extensive use possible would be made of locally procured supplies.

Casualties would be rapidly evacuated to cooler areas such as Maymyo, Kalaw or Taunggyi to speed recovery and consequent recovery of the combat strength of the Army.

The areas under the 15th and 53d Divisions would depend primarily on rail transport. The 33d Division would utilize the 45th Independent Motor Transport Battalion in the evacuation of supplies stored at Kalewa. Materiel would be carried to Kinu by motor trucks and then transferred to rail cars. An independent transport battalion equipped with horse drawn vehicles was also attached to the 33d Division to transport supplies from Monywa to Pakokku, Myingyan and Myinmu.

Operations in Northern Burma [1] (General Reference Map II)

In late July the 18th Division withdrew to the Indaw area and in August and September moved to the vicinity of Namhkan. The 53d Division together with part of the 24th Mixed Brigade conducted delaying operation along the Myitkyina Railway, north of Pinwe, against the British-Indian 36th Division which was not particularly active. Because of air interference with rail traffic, the 53d Division was

---

1. Operations of the 33d Army in northern Burma during the period of the Imphal Operation are covered in Japanese Monograph No. 148, "Burma Operations Record, The 33d Army Operations".

suffering from an acute shortage of supplies of all types. In addition, the Kachin guerrilla force, under control of the enemy, was very active in the area and the strength of the Division was extremely low.

When the 15th Army withdrew from the Imphal area, the United States, British and Chinese armies joined forces in northern Burma. During November the front line extended roughly from Lungling through Bhamo, Indaw, the Zibyu Range and Mawlaik to Kalemyo. As the 15th Army was forced back, its defense lines joined with those of the 33d Army.

The commander of the Burma Area Army, then at Maymyo, determined to secure a line linking Lashio and Mandalay, thence along the Irrawaddy River to Rangoon. In late September, the 15th Army received a warning order to prepare to withdraw to a line linking the Monglong Range, Sagaing and Pakokku. On 3 October, the 53d Division was placed under the 15th Army and orders were received to initiate the first phase of the "Ban" Operation, the withdrawal across the Irrawaddy River.

Command Changes and Plans for the "Ban" Operation

On 30 August, Lt. Gen. Hyotaro Kimura was assigned as commander of the Burma Area Army vice Lt. Gen. Masakazu Kawabe. Lt. Gen. Shihachi Katamura was assigned as commander of the 15th Army replacing Lt. Gen. Mutaguchi. Lt. Gen. Shinichi Tanaka was appointed Chief of Staff, Burma Area Army and Maj. Gen. Gompachi Yoshida, Chief of Staff, 15th Army. On October 10th, General Katamura summoned all chiefs of staff of 15th Army divisions and other major units to Army headquarters at Shwebo to clarify his command policies and assign new divisional missions based on a defensive plan known as the "Ban" Operation:

    1. The 15th Army will take positions along a line linking Katha, Indaw, Pinlebu and Kalewa and while preparing for the move to the Irrawaddy River, will check the enemy in this area. During the preparatory period each unit will make every effort to rebuild its fighting power, re-establish military discipline and restore morale.

    2. Troop disposition during the preparatory period of approximately 50 days will be as follows:

    a. The forward defense line of the 53d Division will be withdrawn to the Pinwe-Auktaw line. The 24th Independent Mixed Brigade will return to its original garrison duty at Moulmein.

    b. The 15th Division will hold its defense positions in the vicinity of Pinbon and Pinlebu and will link up with the 53d Division.

    c. The 33d Division will immediately withdraw to Kalewa, with one element occupying the area around Gangaw to check possible enemy advances through the Kale Valley.

    d. The 31st Division will establish eastwest defense lines at Kanbalu and Shwebo as well as a bridgehead at Sagaing, to cover the main force of the Army.

    3. Following the preparatory period, the withdrawal to the Irrawaddy River and subsequent disposition of the 15th Army will be conducted as follows:

  a. The movement will be started in early December to be completed in approximately 50 days.

  b. The 53d Division will withdraw to Kyaukse along the east bank of the Irrawaddy River and will prepare a final defense position near Meiktila.

  c. The 15th Division will withdraw, through the sector west of the Irrawaddy River, to the area northeast of Shwebo. It will cross the Irrawaddy near Kyaukmyaung and occupy the east bank of the River north of Singu[2], the Monglong Hills (northeast of Mandalay) and will also hold the Kyaukmyaung bridgehead.

  d. The main force of the 33d Division will occupy Monywa, Myingyan and Pakokku. An element will be stationed at Gangaw to hold that position as long as possible.

  e. After covering the withdrawal of the 53d, 15th and 33d Divisions from its positions at Kambalu and Shwebo, the 31st Division will withdraw to defend the bridgehead at Sagaing and the south bank of the Irrawaddy River from Sagaing west to a point opposite Myinmu.

  4. Each division will withdraw vehicles and heavy weapons prior to the general troop withdrawal and will make river crossing preparations. The Army will stock adequate provisions along each route of withdrawal.

  Late in October, the Area Army summoned the chiefs of staff and other staff officers of the 15th, 28th and 33d Armies to Rangoon. Reports were received on the condition of the armies and war exercises

---

 2. Located on the east bank of the Irrawaddy River, east of Shwebo (22°33' N, 96°00 E).

were conducted. In the process of studying the forthcoming operations a number of questions were raised concerning the 15th Army plan for withdrawal to the Irrawaddy River defense line. In consideration of the fact that the 15th Army was facing an enemy of superior strength which had already assumed the offensive, doubts were expressed as to whether or not the present battle line could be held until early December, as specified in the plan. It was also considered doubtful if the Army could accomplish a withdrawal of more than 300 miles and still retain the capability of effecting a redisposition along the east and south banks of the Irrawaddy River.

In refutation of the first objection, the staff of the 15th Army agreed that although the holding of the present positions would be difficult, the Army was in greater danger of suffering internal collapse if the retreat was continued immediately. It was believed that if the present positions could be held for approximately 40 days, reorganization and rebuilding of strength and morale could be accomplished. Furthermore, it was felt necessary to secure the Shwebo Plain and maintain the present battle line until December to permit the 33d Division's withdrawal and evacuation of vital materiel. As far as the second point was concerned, the 15th Army staff were convinced that the withdrawal could be successfully accomplished if the 15th and 53d Divisions moved south along both banks of the Irrawaddy River while the 33d Division withdrew to Monywa through the jungle east of the Chindwin River, avoiding the Shwebo Plain where the 31st

Division was to establish covering positions. To hinder pursuit, bridges on roads which the enemy might use would be demolished as the Army withdrew.

There was also a question raised on which bank of the Irrawaddy River the 15th Army should establish its defensive positions. The answer would, of course, depend on the mission which the Area Army would assign the 15th and the assignment of the mission was, in turn, dependent on the combat strength of the Army and the enemy situation. The Area Army had prepared three principal defensive plans, each contemplating an enemy offensive against the three army fronts. These plans were termed "Dan"(33d Army), "Ban" (15th Army) and "Kan" (28th Army). The appropriate operation would be activated when the enemy offensive was launched and its objectives became clear. Although the enemy main offensive was expected to be launched either against the 15th Army on the Irrawaddy River or against the 28th Army in the southwestern Burma seacoast area, at this time the Area Army had no means of determining where the decisive battle would be fought. In any event, it was absolutely necessary to secure the area along the Irrawaddy from Mandalay to Rangoon. The combat strength of the 15th Army was extremely low and would be even lower at the conclusion of the withdrawal operation. The Army would be faced with directing an operation on a front extending approximately 125 miles, from the Monglong Range (north of Mandalay) to Pakokku, with three reduced strength divisions facing a British-Indian army consisting of about eight divisions.

If the Area Army decided to launch the "Kan" Operation in the 28th Army sector, the 15th Army would be required to secure the strategic line of the Irrawaddy River alone and would undoubtedly be required to hold until the advent of the rainy season in May or June. If the "Ban" Operation should be activated in the 15th Army area, it was realized that the sending of reinforcements by the Area Army would take some time.

If the forces of the 15th Army were to be disposed on the west and north banks of the Irrawaddy, they might become involved in a decisive battle much earlier than would be strategically desirable. In addition, dictated by the nature of the terrain, a defense on the west and north bank of the Irrawaddy would, of necessity, have to be an active defense. With the aid of the natural barrier afforded by the 1,000 or more yard width of the River and with powerful bridgehead defenses established at strategic points, a defense on the east and south banks of the Irrawaddy River could be a passive defense. Since this latter type of defense was more within the capabilities of the 15th Army it was determined to establish the defensive positions behind the water barrier, east and south of the Irrawaddy River.

Another question arose over the defense of the boundary sector between the 15th and 33d Armies against enemy troops invading along the east bank of the Irrawaddy River and the south bank of the Shweli River. The Monglong Mountain Range which marked the northern boundary of the 15th Army area had to be secured to protect its right flank. An enemy element moving from the 33d Army's front had, however, already infiltrated into the Mongmit area while the 33d was preoccupied with the Namhkam front.[3] The 15th Army which was to hold a line from Indaw to the Zibyu Mountain Range until December, lacked sufficient reserves to secure the Mongmit area. It was, therefore, decided that the Mongmit area should be incorporated into the 33d Army operational area, that a force from the 18th Division would repel the enemy already in the area and that the 15th Army would dispatch an element to the sector immediately north of the Monglong Mountains to secure that important area.

Final Plans for the Irrawaddy Battle

At the conclusion of the Rangoon conference, the 15th Army commander made a personal reconnaissance of the hills north of Madaya, the Sagaing area and the Myinmu sector. Upon completing the reconnaissance in December he prepared a plan for the coming Irrawaddy conflict which received the approval of the Burma Area Army.

---

3. See Japanese Monograph No. 148, "Burma Operations Record, The 33d Army Operations".

The 15th Army plan was predicated on the assumption that the enemy would make the major attempt to cross the Irrawaddy in the sector between Myinmu and Kyauktalon, with secondary or divisionary attacks at Singu, Pakokku and Myingyan. It was also expected that the enemy would infiltrate along the east bank of the Irrawaddy and into the Monglong Mountain area in an attempt to disrupt key positions on the right wing of the Army and to drive a wedge between the 15th and 33d Armies. The possibility of a powerful airborne invasion in the Meiktila or Maymyo areas had also to be taken into consideration.

The value of the Irrawaddy River as an obstacle was carefully assessed, taking into consideration the well developed communications network along the river which would facilitate the employment of friendly artillery support.

In the event the Area Army should decide to fight the decisive battle in the 15th Army zone of responsibility, the cooperation of the 33d and 28th Armies could be expected and a minimum of six divisions (including the 2d and 49th Divisions) would participate. By December the recovery of the combat strength of the 15th Army had been more favorable than had been anticipated and it was believed that the combat strength of the 31st, 33d, 15th and 53d Divisions would total 7,000, 5,400, 4,500 and 4,500 men respectively. The number of field pieces was expected to be about 40 per cent of that authorized.

With only one regiment of the India National Army stationed there, the Pakokku area constituted a vulnerable point in the defenses against an enemy approaching from Gangaw. Coordinated action with the 28th Army for the defense of this area was required.

In brief, the 15th Army plan for the defense along the Irrawaddy River was as follows:

    1. The Army will build strong positions on the hill north of Madaya, around Mandalay, at Myinmu and Myingyan and in the delta area northwest of Myingyan. A series of covering positions will also be built north and west of Sagaing. Main positions will be concealed and will be covered by the 15th Division from its Singu defenses, the 31st Division in positions near Shwebo and the 33d Division advance positions near Monywa. Using the positions at Singu, Sagaing and Myinmu as key positions, raiding operations will be carried out against the enemy with a view to diminishing enemy combat strength and obstructing river crossing preparations. If the enemy should attempt a river crossing the front line units will make repeated counterattacks to defeat the enemy on the beach or while actually engaged in the crossing.

    2. In anticipation of enemy airborne invasion forces, key counterattacking positions will be established in strategic positions around Meiktila and Maymyo.

    3. The 15th Division, will occupy positions in depth along a line connecting Singu and a point slightly west of Mongmit, keeping in close contact with the 18th Division. A rear position will be established around the hill northeast of Madaya. Strong advance positions will be built near Kyaukmyaung (west bank of the Irrawaddy River opposite Singu) and a strong element of the Division will occupy the positions in order to harass the enemy and obstruct river crossing preparations.

4. The 31st Division will occupy the bridgehead at Sagaing, the Mandalay perimeter, and the high ground south of Kyauktalon as well as the uplands across the river from Myinmu.

5. The 33d Division will occupy the vicinity of Sameikkon, the upland country around Myingyan, the delta at the confluence of the Irrawaddy and Chindwin Rivers and the key area around Pakokku. A strong advance unit will be deployed in the vicinity of Monywa.

6. The 53d Division will build counterattack positions to be utilized against any enemy airborne raiding force in the Meiktila area. The Main force of the Division will assemble in the Meiktila-Kyaukse sector and make preparations for movement to the Kyauktalon and Singu fronts when needed.

7. One regiment of the Indian National Army will cover both banks of the Irrawaddy River in the vicinity of Nyaungu. The Army artillery unit will emplace elements in the Sagaing area and its main force in the Kyauktalon sector to support the defense of the Sagaing and Myinmu fronts.

8. In the event of an offensive on the Kyauktalon-Myinmu fronts, the main forces of the 31st and 33d Divisions the entire 2d and 53d Divisions, the 14th Tank Regiment, elements of the 18th and 49th Divisions as well as elements of the Army artillery will participate. In the event of an offensive directed against the Singu front, the 15th and 53d Divisions, the 14th Tank Regiment and elements of the Army artillery will participate.

9. Guerrilla units will be deployed in the sectors northwest of Thabeikkyin (northeast of Shwebo) and east of Monywa.

Divisional task forces having been dissolved, the organization of major units of the 15th Army in November 1944 was as follows:

15th DIVISION

    51st Inf Regt
    60th Inf Regt
    67th Inf Regt (less 3d Co)
    21st Fld Arty Regt
    15th Engr Regt

31st DIVISION

    Inf Gp Hq
    58th Inf Regt
    124th Inf Regt
    138th Inf Regt
    31st Mt Arty Regt
    31st Engr Regt
    Elms, 3d Hv Fld Arty Regt
    1st Bn, 21st Fld Arty Regt
    Three AT Btrys
    20th Indep Engr Regt

33d DIVISION

    33d Inf Gp Hq
    213th Inf Regt
    214th Inf Regt
    215th Inf Regt
    33d Mt Arty Regt
    33d Engr Regt

    Elms, 18th Hv Fld Arty Regt
    One plat, 3d Hv Fld Arty Regt
    3d Bn, 2d Fld Arty Regt
    4th Indep Engr Regt
    2d Co, 2d Engr Regt

53d DIVISION

    119th Inf Regt (less 1st Bn)
    128th Inf Regt
    151st Inf Regt
    53d Fld Arty Regt (less 3d Bn)
    53d Engr Regt
    187th Indep Inf Bn

15th Army Situation Prior to the Irrawaddy River Withdrawal

On the 53d Division front, in the vicinity of Mawhun, the British-Indian 36th Division became active about the middle of October and began steadily attacking front line positions. The 53d Division was forced to withdraw to the Pinwe-Auktaw line in late October. Because of persistent enemy air attacks on the Meza Bridge southwest of Indaw, little progress could be made in evacuating the rear echelons of the 53d along the railway line. The Army commander was deeply concerned with the battle situation in that sector because of the reduced combat strength and low morale of the Division.

In early November the 53d Division commander recommended to the 15th Army that the front line in the vicinity of Pinwe, which was becoming increasingly difficult to hold, be abandoned in favor of a line to be established northeast of Wuntho. Fearing that this change would bring about the collapse of the entire battle line and adversely affect the withdrawal operation to be started in December, the Army ordered the 53d Division to hold the existing battle line regardless of personnel losses. The Division was also ordered to execute limited but bold attacks to its front. To relieve the pressure on the 53d Division, the 15th Division was directed to attack the right flank and rear of the enemy 36th Division along the Meza River. Although the attacks of the 15th Division and the counterattacks of the 53d failed to destroy the enemy, they were successful in checking the offensive of the 36th and enabled the 53d Division to hold the line for approximately three weeks. The order to the 53d showed the Division commanders the caliber and determination of the new Army commander and the 53d's success in holding bolstered the sagging combat spirit of the entire 15th Army.

The 33d Division had been subjected since late September to the attacks of the British 5th and 11th Divisions in the sector between Tiddim and Indainggyi. Late in October the 215th Infantry Regiment was sent north of Indainggyi to protect the right flank of the Division. Subsequently the 214th Infantry Regiment, which had defended Tiddim until 17 October and had then conducted delaying actions along the Tiddim-Kalemyo Road, relieved the 215th which withdrew to Monywa on 13 November. In the meantime the enemy 11th Division had moved south through the Kabaw Valley and an element had infiltrated through in an attempt to cut the road between Kalemyo and Kalewa. The main force of the 33d found itself isolated in the Chin Hills under attack from both front and rear. The rear guard unit, consisting of the 214th Infantry Regiment (less the 2d Battalion) and the 2d Battalion, 215th Infantry Regiment and one mountain artillery battery succeeded in breaking through the enemy encirclement and gaining Kalewa in late November.

In the sector around Mawlaik, pressed by the British-Indian 20th Division, which had crossed the Chindwin River in late November, other elements of the 33d Division withdrew to Gonga and held the enemy in check. With its battle line thus shortened, although the Division was fighting against three enemy divisions, it was successful in evacuating much material, including its heavy field guns, through Kalewa and across the Chindwin River.

The 31st Division, after its withdrawal from the Chindwin Valley, dispatched the 138th Infantry Regiment, the 31st Mountain Artillery Regiment (less the 1st and 2d Battalions) and the main strength of the 31st Engineer Regiment to the Sagaing sector to construct bridgehead and covering positions. The 58th Infantry Regiment was given the mission of holding the positions at Kanbalu, under direct command of the 15th Army. The Division assembled the main forces of all other line units in the Shwebo sector and established defense positions. In early October the 31st was assigned the mission of holding the Shwebo sector as long as possible, to delay the advance of the enemy and gain time for defense preparations along the Irrawaddy River. At the same time it was to cover the withdrawal of the 15th and 33d Divisions from the areas along the Myitkyina Railway and the Tiddim-Kalewa Road.

As the dry season arrived, enemy attacks mounted in fury along the entire front. In spite of intensive efforts of the 33d Army, superior enemy forces captured the Bhamo garrison in mid-October and was driving on the Myitson area. The 33d Army ordered the main force of the 18th Division to attack the enemy at Myitson. At the same time the Area Army ordered the 2d Division, which was withdrawing to south Burma, to be ready for action in the Mandalay and Maymyo sectors.

Pressure on the 53d Division also increased and when enemy elements infiltrated into the gap between the 53d and 15th Divisions in late November, the 15th Army ordered the 53d to withdraw to Katha and the sector north of Tigyaing. The 15th Division was ordered to withdraw its right wing to maintain contact with the revised battle line of the 53d Division.

The British-Indian 19th Division began an assault against the 15th Division in late November. In the Kalewa sector, the enemy 11th and 20th Divisions also attacked and pursued the 33d Division which was forced to withdraw from the west side of the Chindwin River to the Mutaik and Shwegyin areas on 2 December. The enemy continued to press forward and also moved into the Mutaik and Shwegyin areas.

Withdrawal to the Irrawaddy Defense Line

The 15th Army issued orders to the 53d and 15th Divisions directing the commencement of the withdrawal movement to the Irrawaddy River line on 1 December. The 33d Division was directed to withdraw on 4 December, giving the Division additional time for disposal of munitions in its area.

The 213th Infantry Regiment, acting as rear guard of the 33d Division, checked the enemy in the Shwegyin-Mutaik sector and endeavored to remove munitions from that sector. The main force of the Division departed Mutaik in mid-December and withdrew toward Monywa through Yeu. The 213th Infantry attempted to check the enemy in the vicinity of

Pyingaing and also in Paga but was not successful. In mid-December the Army rushed the 124th Infantry Regiment (less one battalion) of the 31st Division from Shwebo to Pyingaing. With the assistance of the 5th Air Division, the 124th was successful in aiding the 213th Infantry Regiment to disengage from the enemy. In late December and early January the 33d Division completed its withdrawal to the vicinity of Monywa.

The 53d Division deployed covering units in the vicinity of Inywa and Meza, while the 15th Division deployed similar units at Wuntho and several key points to the west. Early in December, both divisions began withdrawing without being detected by the enemy. The main force of the 53d Division turned to the east bank of the Irrawaddy River at Katha, Tigyaing and Male and then moved south toward Mandalay. The rear guard of the 53d Division was pursued by an element of the British 36th Division along the east bank of the Irrawaddy although little contact was experienced.

The main force of the 15th Division advanced toward the northeast side of Shwebo, through Kawlin, with the enemy in close pursuit. The 60th Infantry Regiment, which had been fighting in the sector west of Pinlebu, disengaged from the enemy about December 20th and withdrew via Okkan and Kanbalu, protecting the rear of the Division. The British-Indian 19th Division had apparently crossed the Chindwin River near Paungbyin and advanced to the Wuntho sector. The 15th Division, aided by the covering units of the 31st Division at Kanbalu and Thabeikkyin, was able to move to its destination in early January.

After accomplishing its mission of covering the retreat of the 15th and 53d Divisions, the 31st Division was attacked, in late December, by the British-Indian 2d and 19th Divisions. Fierce fighting took place beginning 26 December along the entire Shwebo Plain advance line from Kanbalu to Yeu.

About the 7th of January, a strong enemy force approached the main positions in the Shwebo area and another enemy group stood ready to encircle the right flank of the Division. Anticipating an all-out attack by two divisions within a matter of days, the 31st Division commander was faced with deciding whether to stand at Shwebo and probably incur heavy losses or to withdraw to the stronger defensive positions beyond the Irrawaddy River. On 8 January, key points of the Division's positions were subjected to heavy mortar fire and air bombings. On that same day, Colonel Tetsujiro Tanaka, a 15th Army staff officer, arrived from Maymyo with orders to halt defensive operations at Shwebo and prepare for immediate withdrawal to the Irrawaddy. Emphasis was placed on defending the bridgehead at Sagaing in order that the enemy should not capitalize on the shift and seize that vital point. The retreat of the 31st Division was started at once.

MAP NO. 21

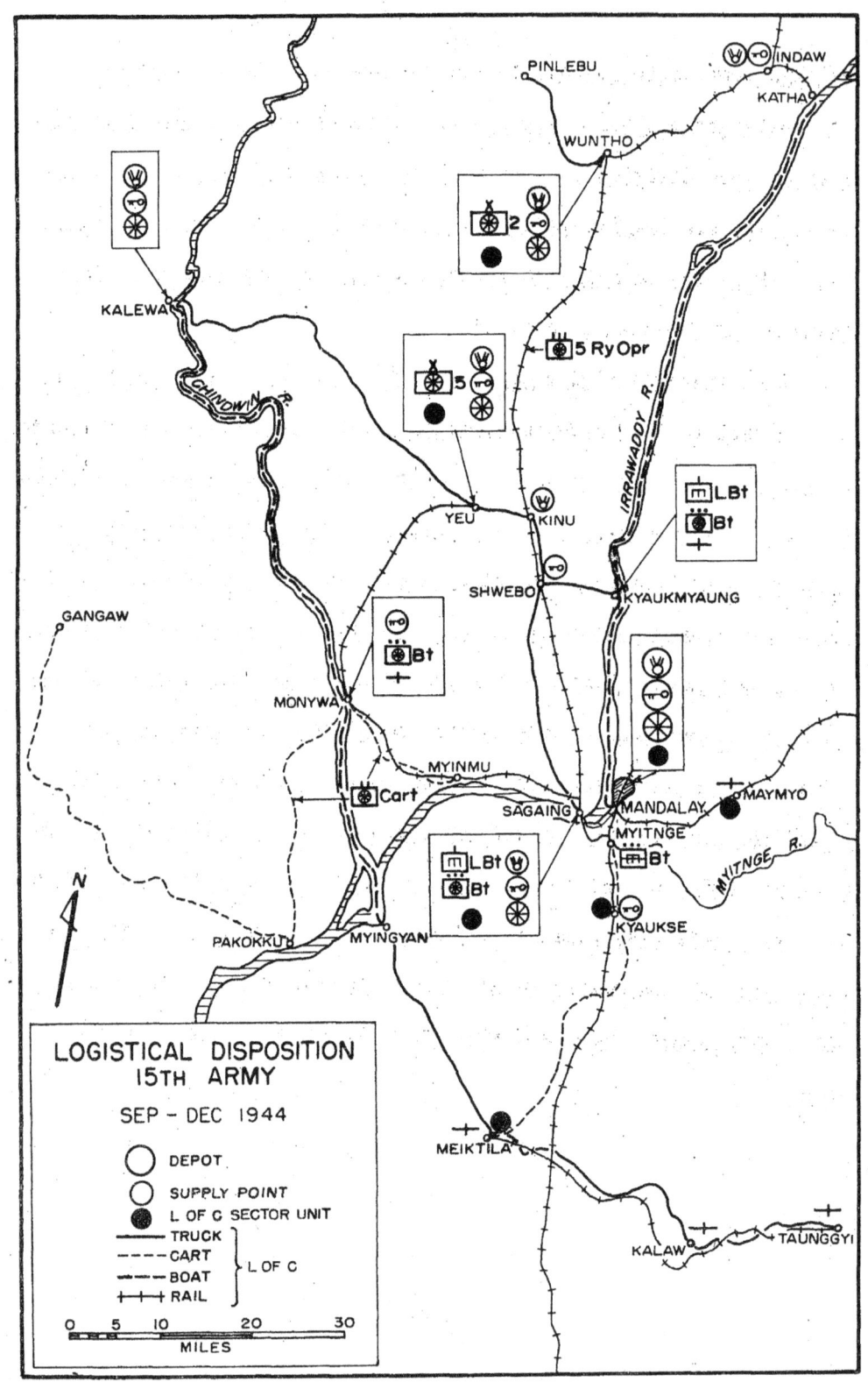

Logistics in the 15th Army Withdrawal (Map No. 21)

The Mandalay Sector Transport Command was charged with control of the rear disposition in the Mandalay and Sagaing sectors. Other transport units, as well as the greater part of the supply depots under Army command were assigned to the Command. In the Sagaing sector, military supplies required for the 31st Division (rations and forage for two months and ammunition for approximately one month) were disposed and the remainder was dispersed to Mandalay, Tonbo, Myitnge, Kyaukse and Meiktila.

Logistic operations were based on the following schedule: The withdrawal from Indaw, Wuntho, Kalewa and Yeu to be accomplished by mid-October; withdrawal from Kinu and Monywa by mid-November; redisposition in the Sagaing and Mandalay sectors by mid-December. Due to the interruption of railway transport by enemy air activity, logistic operations were extremely difficult. The 5th Railway Regiment was called on to perform virtual miracles of repair and maintenance of rail facilities and railroad operations continued. The evacuation of casualties and munitions along the routes of retreat a and the delivery of munitions at the new positions was generally completed by late November. Evacuation from the Kalewa sector was, however, delayed until the end of December.

Destruction of airfields at Shwebo, Wuntho and Kawlin, and the removal of rails from the Myitkyina Railway in the sector north of Shwebo were generally completed prior to the withdrawal.

By the 1st of January 1945, the withdrawal, re-disposition and reorganization of the 15th Army rear units was completed.

Construction of Irrawaddy Defense Positions

The middle of January found virtually all units of the 15th Army in defensive positions along the Irrawaddy. The construction of the defenses had, however, been slower than had been anticipated. In the Monglong Hills, north of Madaya, and at Kyaukmyaung on the 15th Division front, except for some simple field positions, defenses were still in the planning stage. Around Meiktila, which the 53d Division has been assigned to fortify, positions were still in the reconnaissance stage. The 31st Division had completed 60 to 70 per cent of the positions covering the Sagaing approaches and had established a fairly strong field defense complex. Construction of infantry positions in all other 31st Division areas was about 30 per cent completed while heavy gun positions were approximately 50 per cent completed. The 33d Division had constructed simple field positions in the vicinity of Monywa and only skeleton positions had been built by the INA at Pakokku and Myingyan.

The construction and repair of roads and waterworks had just been started.

Military discipline and morale had, however, improved vastly under the new commanders and the units faced the future with full confidence in their ability to hold the Irrawaddy line and drive the enemy back.

The Irrawaddy Battle and the subsequent withdrawal of the 15th, 28th and 33d Armies from Burma are covered in Monographs 59, 132 and 148.

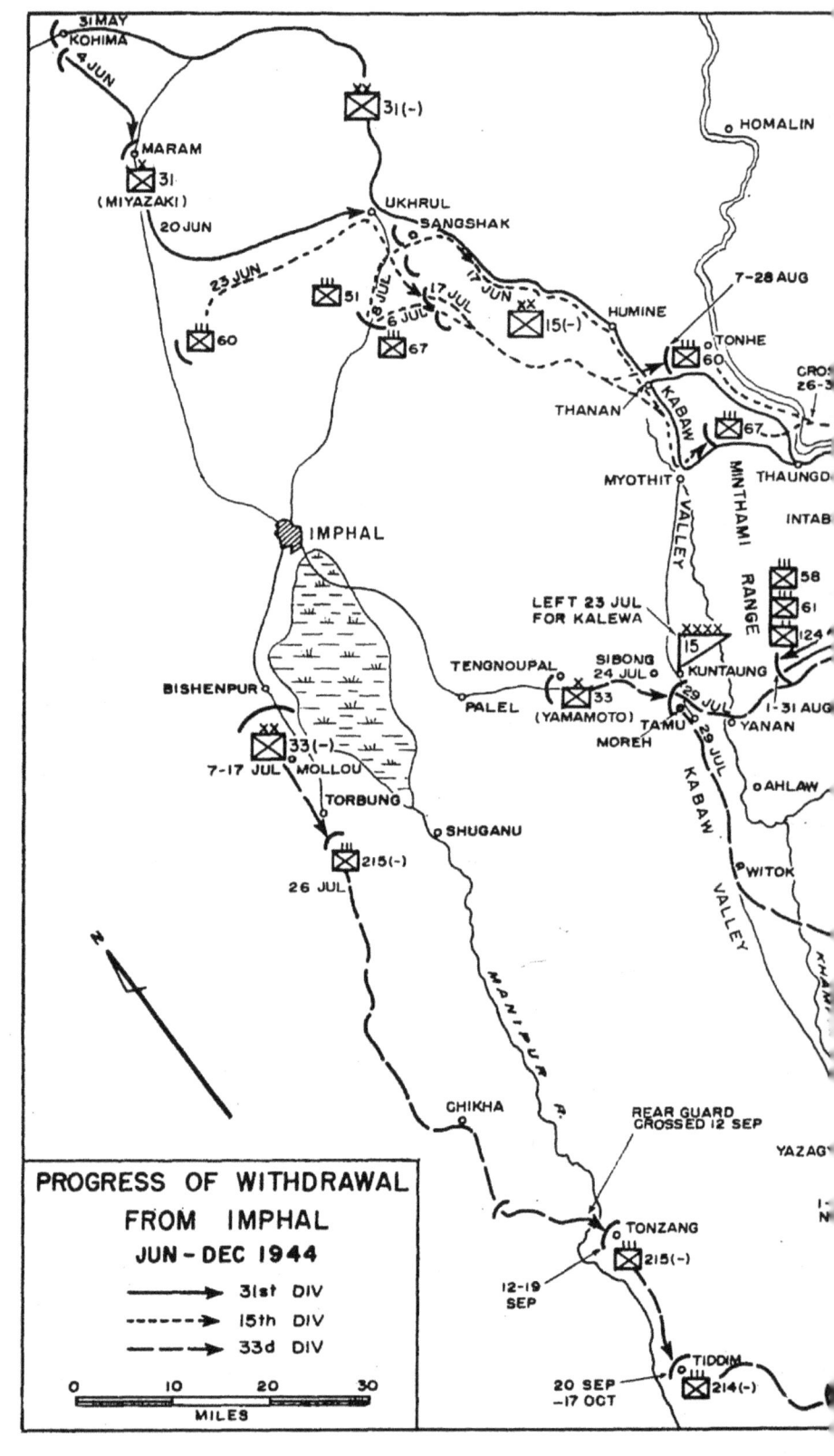

GENERAL REFERENCE MAP NO. I

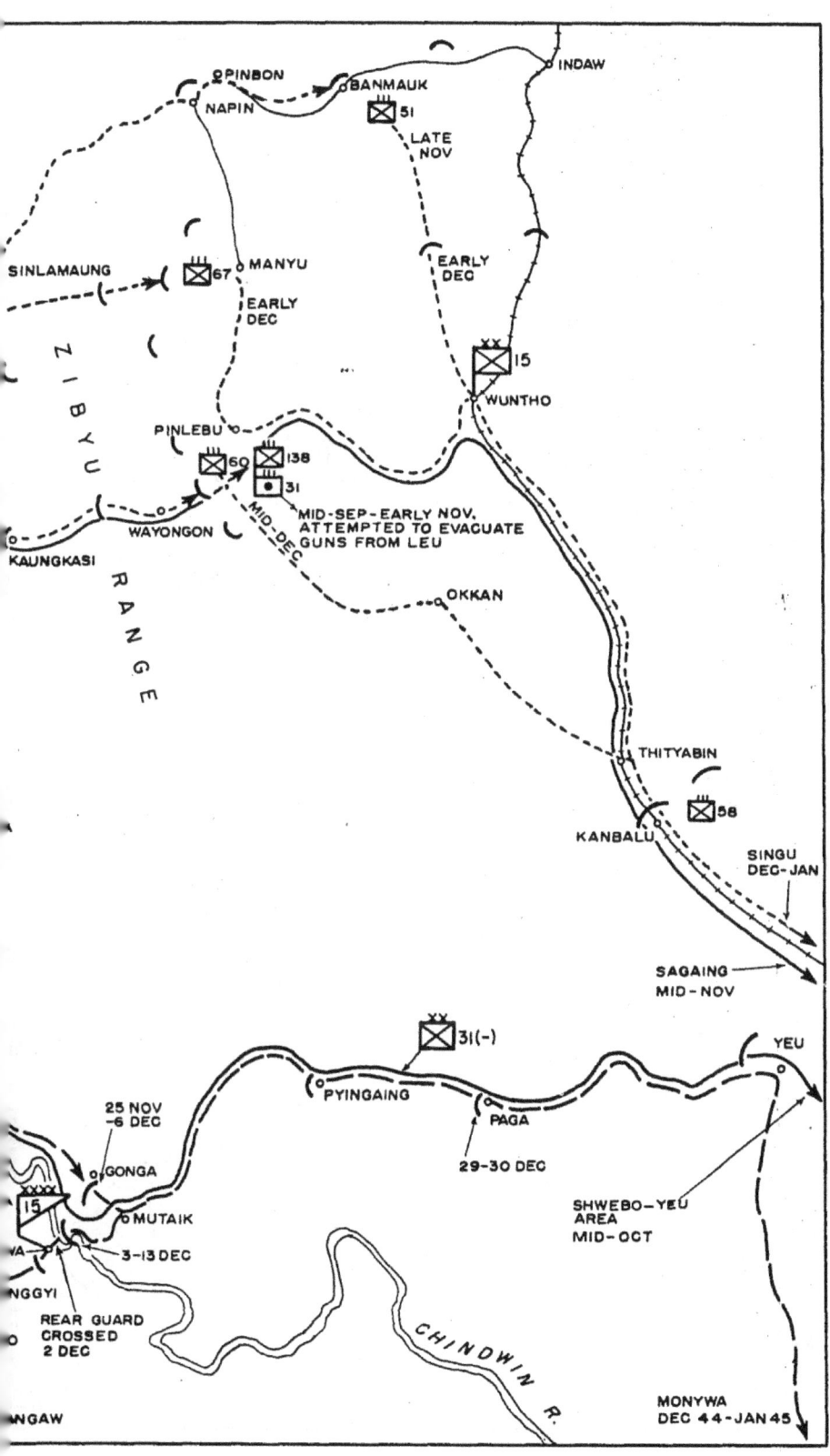

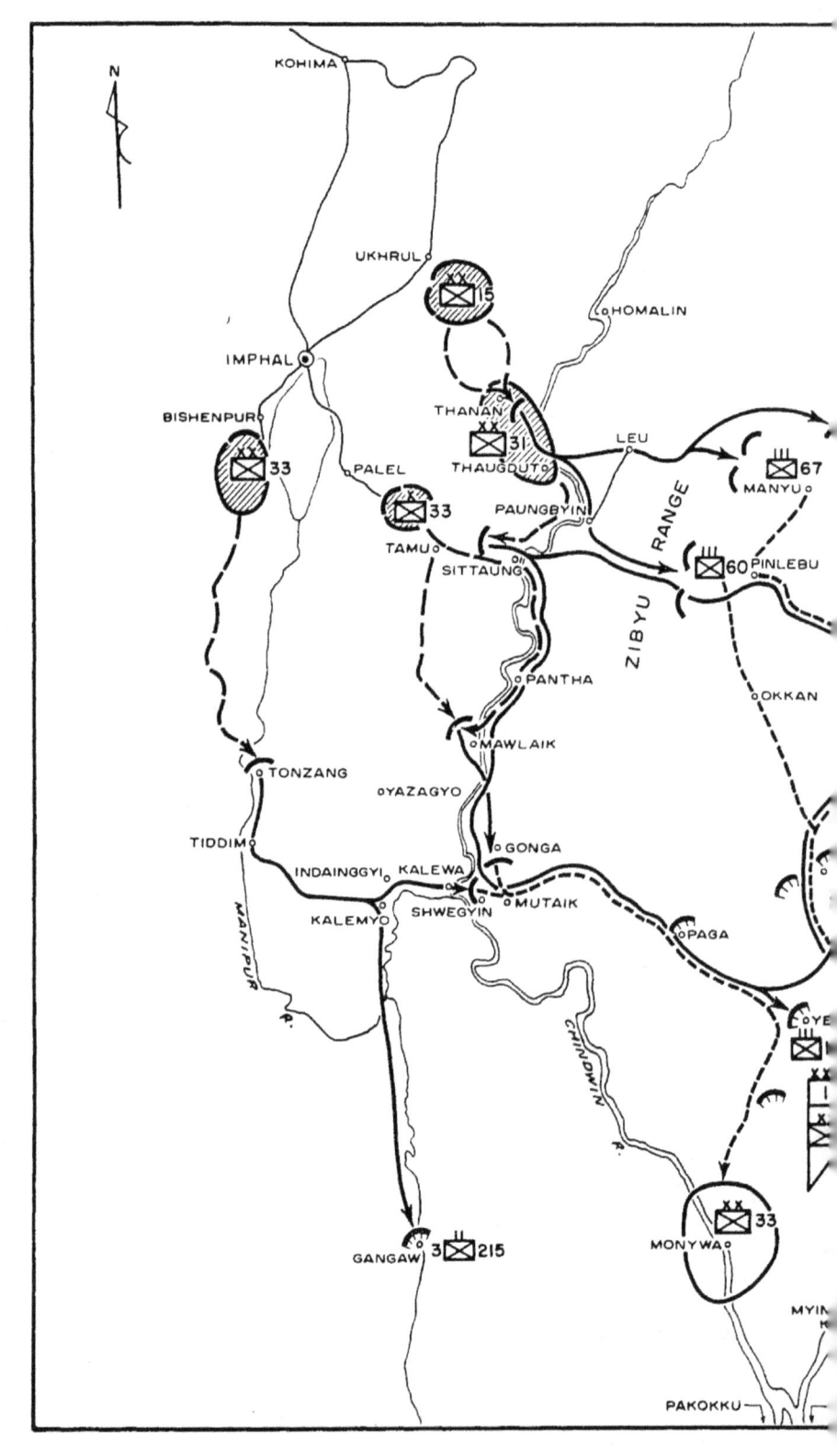

GENERAL REFERENCE MAP NO. II

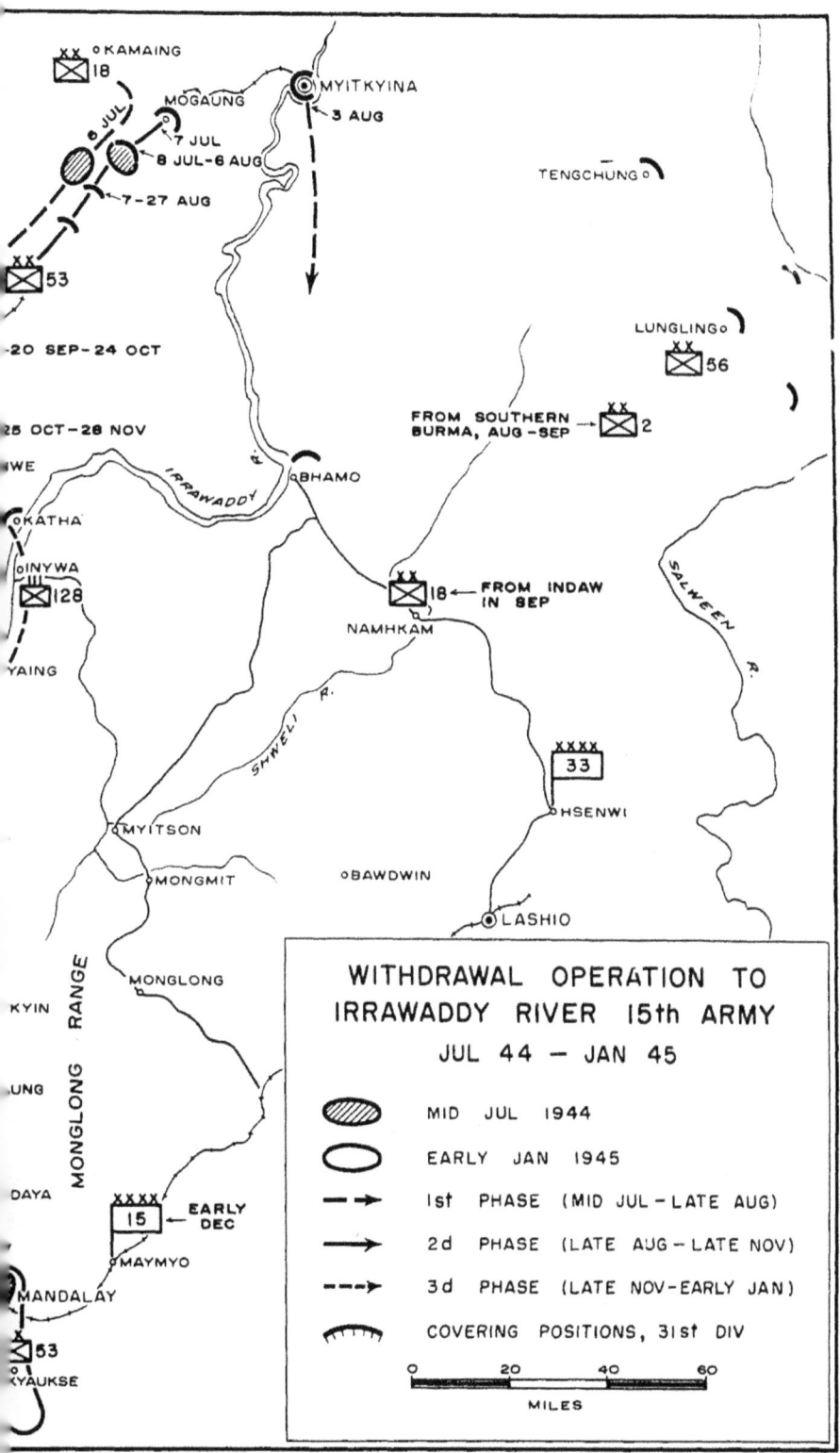

www.ingramcontent.com/pod-product-compliance
Lightning Source LLC
Chambersburg PA
CBHW080503110426
42742CB00017B/2980